Scotland's Gardens Scheme 94

Contents

FRONT COVER PHOTOGRAPH
Paeonia suffruticosa subsp. rockii Haw & Lauener
This beautiful tree peony was originally brought into cultivation as seed collected from plants in a monastery garden in Gansu, China by Joseph Rock.
The plant shown here is at Logan Botanic Garden near Stranraer, Wigtownshire.
Photograph by Sidney J Clarke, ARPS
Principal Photographer at the Royal Botanic Garden, Edinburgh

---

Printed by Alna Limited, Broxburn West Lothian

Charity No. SC 011337   ISSN No. 0967-831X   ISBN No. 0-901549-08-8

CHAIRMAN'S MESSAGE

This year we have altered the layout of the handbook which will hopefully enable you to find our gardens more easily. We have also shown which gardens are suitable for wheelchairs by adding the internationally recognised wheelchair symbol alongside the garden name.

Each entry also clearly shows the Owners' choice of charity to which up to 40% of the gross takings may be given. It is perhaps worth noting that if an Owner selects a medical or cancer related charity then, because the Queen's Nursing Institute (Scotland) is one of our principal beneficiaries, over 70% of the day's takings will be donated to medical charities.

I am sure you will enjoy reading this handbook and choosing which gardens to visit, and why not take a friend or two along with you so that the good name of the Gardens Scheme can spread even further around Scotland.

All our Owners work so hard to ensure that their gardens are at their best for you to see and by maintaining our high standards, you will have a treat in store. My thanks go to them, all our Organisers and the many helpers behind the scenes who make the openings run so smoothly, and finally to you, the members of the public, who help to keep this happy charity going each year.

Barbara J. Findlay

SCOTLAND'S GARDENS SCHEME HISTORY

Scotland's Gardens Scheme was founded on 23rd March 1931 at a garden owners' meeting called to help raise £2,000 which the Queen's Nursing Institute needed to fund the rapid expansion of district nursing. The Queen Mother, then the Duchess of York, lent her support, while King George V promised that the Balmoral gardens would open for the Scheme, with a generous annual contribution still being made today.

Under the inaugural chairmanship of the Countess of Minto, a central committee with a network of volunteer organisers throughout Scotland was formed, much the shape of the Scheme today. £1,000 was raised in the first year, double that in the next, and by 1939 over £22,000 was contributed in one shilling entrance fees. Even during the war years the proceeds increased, helped by flower and plant stalls, and through the provision of teas – without sugar.

Although the training duties of the Queen's Nursing Institute were taken over by the National Health Service, many elderly nurses then and now still receive our support. In 1952 the Gardens Fund of the National Trust for Scotland became our other main beneficiary, so that we could help to preserve the many gardens of historical importance in Scotland. Both our principal beneficiaries have contributed articles to this handbook, explaining in detail how important our contributions are to them and for what purposes they are used.

In 1961 it was agreed that all Garden Owners might select a registered charity to which up to 40% of the gross takings from their garden opening could be donated. This benefits over 150 different charities each year and is unique to Scotland's Gardens Scheme.

Over the years Scotland's Gardens Scheme has enabled millions of people to enjoy the beautiful and often 'never before seen' gardens of Scotland – with your help we hope that this will continue for many years to come.

A MESSAGE FROM
THE QUEEN'S NURSING INSTITUTE, SCOTLAND

At the Annual General Meeting, Lady Prosser sincerely thanked all those whose work had made the presentation of a cheque for £38,652 possible in order to assist the Institute to carry out its work. As a result of discussions with Scotland's Gardens Scheme, this year the Queen's Nursing Institute, Scotland, is directing this generous donation to contribute towards

NURSING CARE in the HOME

Three schemes are being set up to provide

* Regular nursing assistance for patients with both mental and physical disabilities who are being cared for at home.

(Project in Lothian area
in co-operation with CROSSROADS)

* Assistance at home caring for those in the terminal stages of Motor Neurone Disease

(Project in the West of Scotland
in co-operation with MARIE CURIE CANCER CARE SCOTLAND
and the SCOTTISH MOTOR NEURONE DISEASE ASSOCIATION)

* A Support Nurse for stroke patients in south Glasgow. To be a focus of the rehabilitation programme for the patient and to assist relatives

(in co-operation with the
CHEST, HEART & STROKE ASSOCIATION)

The cost of these schemes will be
£70,000 in the next year

A leaflet giving further details of these projects and the work of the Queen's Nursing Institute, Scotland, is available on request from

The Queen's Nursing Institute, Scotland
31 Castle Terrace
Edinburgh EH1 2EL

♔ The National Trust for Scotland

It is a great pleasure for me to be able to use this annual message to thank all those owners of private gardens in Scotland who open their gates to the public and contribute so much to so many charities, not just our own.

Beautiful gardens can often hide the hours of dedication and hard work (come rain or shine) that caring owners devote to their creation and maintenance. Apart from one or two similarities here and there, they are all different. Different shapes, different sizes and different plants - that is what makes them such a joy to visit. The variety is enormous and exciting.

The weather, generally, was not kind to gardens, or gardeners, in 1993. I congratulate each one of you on achieving such high standards and for giving those of us who were your visitors so much pleasure and such a fascinating insight into what can be achieved, with a little help from Mother Nature!

The National Trust for Scotland has initiated a series of open days throughout the country to invite Scotland's Gardens Scheme garden owners to visit our properties and to see that the money so generously donated to the Trust each year is being used wisely and carefully. Garden owners know only too well that this is a hobby that can cost a great deal. That is why we are so deeply appreciative of the financial assistance given to us by Scotland's Gardens Scheme. It enables us to carry out each year many garden projects which would otherwise have to be postponed or cancelled, to the detriment of the great gardens managed by the Trust for the benefit of the nation.

The Scheme's donation to the Trust in previous years has been spent entirely in helping to run our gardens. In response to suggestions by your Executive Committee, we have agreed to use income from this year's opening at Trust properties to help sponsor a horticulture student at Threave. I am sure you will all agree that training young gardeners properly is essential for the future of gardens in Scotland and the National Trust for Scotland is delighted to play its part in bringing that about.

I hope you all have a successful gardening year in 1994.

Douglas Dow
Director

THE GARDENERS'
ROYAL BENEVOLENT SOCIETY IN SCOTLAND

The Gardeners' Royal Benevolent Society opened Netherbyres in 1993 as a residence for retired gardeners and their spouses.

The house is run on Abbeyfield lines, with a Warden providing two meals a day. All rooms have en suite facilities and there is a lift. Greenhouses are being erected and these will give much pleasure to the residents.

Netherbyres is on the outskirts of Eyemouth, where there are many facilities.

The Society would like to hear of any retired gardener or their spouse who is in need of accommodation or financial assistance. In the first instance please contact Miss May Wardlaw, Rosemount, Ecclesmachan Road, Uphall, Broxburn, West Lothian EH52 6JR, the Society's Regional Organiser for Scotland.

Scotland's Gardens Scheme has strongly supported this Society for many years and this regular income is much appreciated. Donations are warmly welcomed.

C. R. C. Bunce, Secretary-Administrator, The Gardeners' Royal Benevolent Society, Bridge House, 139 Kingston Road, Leatherhead, Surrey KT22 7NT

THE ROYAL GARDENERS' ORPHAN FUND
Charity No: 248746

We are currently assisting seven orphaned children on a regular basis in Scotland and over the past year have also helped a significant number of needy children who have a parent employed full time in a horticultural capacity.

Four of these children became eligible for assistance last year when their father, a head gardener, died at the age of thirty eight. The youngest of the children was only 10 months old at the time of his father's death, and it is due to the regular support of organisations such as yourselves that we feel able to take on such long term commitments.

Applications from families in need in Scotland have increased considerably over the past two years. For example, we have helped one couple with the provision of winter clothing for their five- and three-year-old daughters. The father, still a young man, is unlikely to ever work again after extensive surgery following cancer of the bowel. It has been discovered that the form of cancer he has can be hereditary and consequently his young daughters will have to undertake regular screening to ensure they remain clear of the disease.

May we take this opportunity of thanking the many supporters of Scotland's Gardens Scheme whose support makes us able to continue our work.

48 St Alban's Road, Codicote, Herts SG4 8UT Tel: (0438) 820783

GENERAL INFORMATION

Houses are not open unless specifically stated; where the house, or part of the house is shown an additional charge is usually made.

Lavatories. Private gardens do not normally have outside lavatories. Regrettably, for security reasons, owners have been advised not to admit visitors into their houses to use inside toilets.

Dogs. Unless otherwise stated, dogs are usually admitted, but only <u>if kept on a lead</u>. Dogs are not admitted to houses.

Tea. When tea is available at a garden opening this is indicated in the text.

Professional Photographers. No photographs taken in a garden may be used for sale or reproduction without prior permission of the garden owner.

& Denotes gardens suitable for wheelchairs.

# Denotes gardens opening for the first time or re-opening after several years.

National Trust for Scotland. Members are requested to note that where a National Trust property has allocated an opening day to Scotland's Gardens Scheme which is one of its own normal opening days, members can gain entry on production of their Trust membership card (although donations to Scotland's Gardens Scheme will be most welcome).

Children. All children must be accompanied by an adult.

SCOTLAND'S GARDENS SCHEME

Scotland's Gardens Scheme welcomes gardens of all sizes. If you would like further information on how to open your garden on behalf of our charity, please contact the General Organiser at the address given below.

To: THE GENERAL ORGANISER, SCOTLAND'S GARDENS SCHEME,
        31 CASTLE TERRACE, EDINBURGH EH1 2EL Telephone: 031 229 1870

Please send further information on how to open my garden for Scotland's Gardens Scheme to the address below.

NAME & ADDRESS: (Block capitals please)

....

....

....

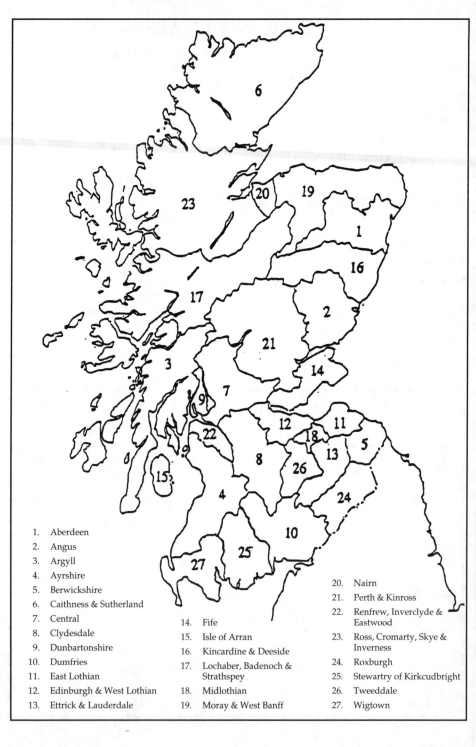

1. Aberdeen
2. Angus
3. Argyll
4. Ayrshire
5. Berwickshire
6. Caithness & Sutherland
7. Central
8. Clydesdale
9. Dunbartonshire
10. Dumfries
11. East Lothian
12. Edinburgh & West Lothian
13. Ettrick & Lauderdale
14. Fife
15. Isle of Arran
16. Kincardine & Deeside
17. Lochaber, Badenoch & Strathspey
18. Midlothian
19. Moray & West Banff
20. Nairn
21. Perth & Kinross
22. Renfrew, Inverclyde & Eastwood
23. Ross, Cromarty, Skye & Inverness
24. Roxburgh
25. Stewartry of Kirkcudbright
26. Tweeddale
27. Wigtown

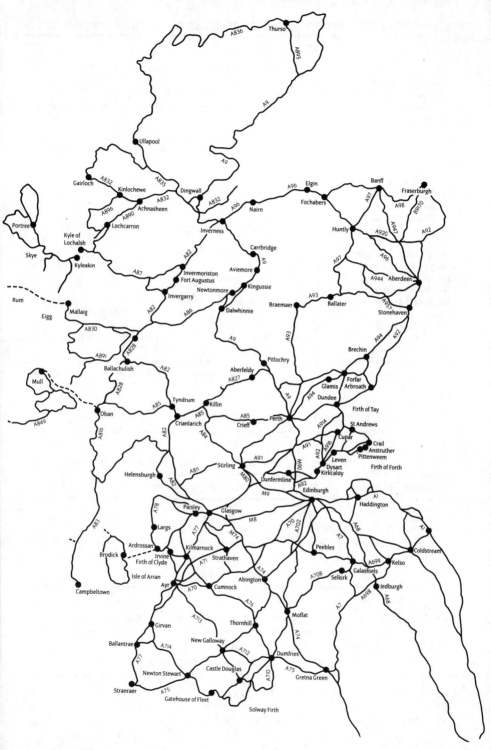

THE GARDENS LISTED BELOW OPEN ON A REGULAR BASIS, OR BY APPOINTMENT.

ABERDEEN

23 Don Street, Old Aberdeen   *Daily April – October by appointment: 0224 487269*
Kildrummy Castle Gardens, Alford   *Daily April – October*
Pitmedden Garden, Pitmedden   *Daily 1 May – 30 September 10am-5.30pm*

ANGUS

House of Pitmuies, Guthrie, by Forfar   *Daily 1 April – 31 October 10am-5pm*

ARGYLL

Achnacloich, Connel   *Daily 3 April-26 June and 2 August-31 October 10am-6pm*
An Cala, Ellenabeich, Isle of Seil   *Daily 9 March-30 September 10am-6pm*
Ardchattan Priory, North Connel   *Daily 1 April-30 October 9 am-9pm*
Ardkinglas Woodland Garden, Cairndow   *Open all year*
Ardmaddy Castle, Balvicar, by Oban   *Daily 15 March-31 October or by appointment: 08523 353*
Barguillean's "Angus Garden", Taynuilt   *Open all year*
Coille Dharaich, Kilmelford   *Open by appointment: 08522 285*
Crarae Glen Garden, Minard, Inveraray   *Daily April-October 9am-6pm. Winter daylight hours*
Dalnaheish, Tayvallich, Lochgilphead   *April-October by appointment: 05467 286*
Druimavuic House, Appin   *Daily 17 April-2 July 10am-6pm*
Druimneil House, Port Appin   *Daily 28 March-19 June 9am-6pm*
Glenfeochan House Hotel, Kilmore, by Oban   *Daily 15 March-31 October 10-6pm*
Jura House, Ardfin, Isle of Jura   *Open all year 9am-5pm*
Kinlochlaich House Gardens, Appin   *Open all year (except Suns mid Oct-March) 9.30am-5.30pm*
Tighnamara, Melfort, Kilmelford   *Spring-Autumn by appointment: 08522 224*
Torosay Castle & Gardens, Isle of Mull   *Open all year Summer: 9am-7pm Winter: Sunrise-Sunset*

AYRSHIRE

Blair, Dalry   *All year round*
Culzean Castle & Country Park,   *Daily April-October 10.30am-5.30pm*

BERWICKSHIRE

Bughtrig, near Leitholm   *Open daily May-September 11am-5pm or by appointment: 0890 840678*
Manderston, Duns   *Sundays & Thursdays 5 May-29 September 2-5.30pm*
The Hirsel, Coldstream   *Open daily all year reasonable daylight hours*

CENTRAL

Blairhoyle, Port of Menteith   *Wednesdays April-September 1-5pm*

DUMBARTON

Glenarn, Rhu   *Daily 21 March-21 June Sunrise to Sunset*

DUMFRIES

Arbigland, Kirkbean   *Tuesdays-Sundays: May-September 2-6pm Also Bank Holiday Mondays*

EAST LOTHIAN

Shepherd House, Inveresk   *Thursday 5 May-Sunday 8 May 2-5.30pm*

EDINBURGH & WEST LOTHIAN

Kirknewton House, Kirknewton   *Sunday 5 June-Friday 10 June 2-6pm*
Newliston, Kirkliston   *Wednesdays-Sundays 4 May-5 June 2-6pm*

FIFE
Cambo House, Kingsbarns *Daily all year 10am-4pm*

KINCARDINE & DEESIDE
Shooting Greens, Strachan *Monday 25 April-Sunday 15 May or by appointment: 0330 850221*

LOCHABER, BADENOCH & STRATHSPEY
Ardtornish, Lochaline *Daily 1 April-31 October 10am-6pm*

MIDLOTHIAN
Arniston, Gorebridge *Tuesdays, Thursdays & Sundays July-mid September*
Greenfield Lodge, Lasswade *First Tuesdays in March-September 2-5pm or by appointment: 031 663 9338 the day before*

PERTH AND KINROSS
Auchleeks House, Calvine *Wednesdays 22 June-3 August 2 – 5pm*
Bolfracks, Aberfeldy *Daily 1 April-31 October 10am-6pm*
Cluny House Gardens, Aberfeldy *Daily 1 March-31 October 10am-6pm*
Dowhill, Cleish *Thursdays in May and June 1.30-4pm*
Scone Palace, Perth *1 April-10 October: weekdays 9.30am-5pm Sundays 1.30pm-5pm July & August: 10am-5pm*
Lude, Blair Atholl *Thursdays 16 June-11 August (excl.30 June) 11am-5pm*

RENFREW, INVERCLYDE & EASTWOOD
Church Street, Kilbarchan *17 April-4 September (excl.July) Tuesdays, Thursdays, most weekends by appointment: 05057 03282*
Knapps, Kilmacolm *March-September weekdays by appointment: 0505 87 2774 daytime*

ROSS, CROMARTY, SKYE & INVERNESS
Abriachan Garden Nursery, Loch Ness side *Daily 9-dusk*
Brin School Fields, Flichity *Daily June-September 8.30am-7pm Sundays 2-5pm*
Aigas House & Field Centre, by Beauly *Daily May-September*
Dunvegan Castle, Isle of Skye *Daily 21 March-29 October 10am-5pm*
Glamaig, Portree, Isle of Skye *Daily Easter to mid-September*
Leckmelm Shrubbery & Arboretum, by Ullapool *Daily 1 April-30 September 10am-6pm*
Sea View, Dundonnell *Easter to mid-October 10am-dusk*

ROXBURGH
Floors Castle, Kelso *Easter weekend & 24-28 April, May, June & September: Sunday-Thursdays. July & August: open daily. October: Sundays & Wednesdays 10.30am-4.30pm*

STEWARTRY OF KIRKCUDBRIGHT
Corsock House, Castle Douglas *Open by appointment*
Southwick House, Dumfries *27 June-3 July afternoons*

TWEEDDALE
Kailzie Gardens, Peebles *Daily 25 March-30 October 11am-5.30pm*

WIGTOWN
Ardwell House Gardens, Ardwell *Daily 1 March-31 October 10am-6pm*
Castle Kennedy & Lochinch Gardens *Daily 1 April-30 September 10am-5pm*
Galloway House Gardens, Garlieston *Daily 1 March-31 October 9am-5pm*
Whitehills, Newton Stewart *Daily 1 April-31 October by appointment: 0671 402049*

MONTHLY CALENDAR LIST

FEBRUARY *For regular openings see pages 10 and 11*

SUNDAY 20th FEBRUARY
RENFREW, INVERCLYDE & EASTWOOD...... **ARDGOWAN,** Inverkip   2 – 5pm

SUNDAY 27th FEBRUARY (provisionally)
FIFE .... **CAMBO HOUSE,** Kingsbarns   2 – 5pm

MARCH *For regular openings see pages 10 and 11*

TUESDAY 1st MARCH
MIDLOTHIAN .... **GREENFIELD LODGE,** Lasswade   2 – 5pm

SUNDAY 6th MARCH
MIDLOTHIAN .... **PRESTONHALL,** Pathhead   2 – 5pm

SUNDAY 13th MARCH
CENTRAL .... **KILBRYDE CASTLE,** Dunblane   2 – 4pm
MIDLOTHIAN .... **GREENFIELD LODGE,** Lasswade   2 – 4.30pm

SUNDAY 27th MARCH
MIDLOTHIAN .... **GREENFIELD LODGE,** Lasswade   2 – 4.30pm

APRIL *For regular openings see pages 10 and 11*

SUNDAY 3rd APRIL
AYRSHIRE .... **CARNELL,** Hurlford   2 – 4.30pm

TUESDAY 5th APRIL
MIDLOTHIAN .... **GREENFIELD LODGE,** Lasswade   2 – 5pm

SUNDAY 10th APRIL
AYRSHIRE .... **CULZEAN CASTLE &**
                                                        COUNTRY PARK   10.30am – 5.30pm
CENTRAL .... **KILBRYDE CASTLE,** Dunblane   2 – 5pm
DUMBARTON... **OLD COURT,** Rhu   2 – 5pm
DUMFRIES .... **BARJARG TOWER,** Auldgirth   2 – 5pm
EDINBURGH & WEST LOTHIAN .... **DEAN GARDENS & ANN STREET,**
                                                        Edinburgh   2 – 6pm

FIFE	**CAMBO,** Kingsbarns	2 – 5pm
RENFREW, INVERCLYDE & EASTWOOD	**FINLAYSTONE,** Langbank	2 – 5pm
ROXBURGH	**MONTEVIOT,** Jedburgh	2 – 5pm

SUNDAY 17th APRIL

ABERDEEN	**AUCHMACOY,** Ellon	1.30 – 4.30pm
BERWICKSHIRE	**NETHERBYRES,** Eyemouth	2 – 6pm
EAST LOTHIAN	**WINTON HOUSE,** Pencaitland	2 – 6pm
MIDLOTHIAN	**ARNISTON,** Gorebridge	2 – 5.30pm

SATURDAY 23rd APRIL

EDINBURGH & WEST LOTHIAN	**DOUGLAS CRESCENT GARDENS,** Edinburgh	2 – 5pm

SATURDAY & SUNDAY 23rd & 24th APRIL

EAST LOTHIAN	**DIRLETON VILLAGE**	2 – 6pm

SUNDAY 24th APRIL

ETTRICK & LAUDERDALE	**BEMERSYDE,** Melrose	2 – 6pm
FIFE	**THE MURREL,** Aberdour	10am – 5pm
KINCARDINE & DEESIDE	**SHOOTING GREENS,** Strachan	2 – 5pm
MORAY & WEST BANFF	**BALLINDALLOCH CASTLE**	10am – 5pm
TWEEDDALE	**NETHERURD HOUSE,** Blyth Bridge	2 – 6pm

WEDNESDAY 27th APRIL

CENTRAL	**NORRIESTON HOUSE,** Thornhill	2 – 5.30pm

SATURDAY 30th APRIL

ROSS, CROMARTY, SKYE & INVERNESS	**INVEREWE,** Poolewe	9.30am – sunset

---

MAY *For regular openings see pages 10 and 11*

SUNDAY 1st MAY

BERWICKSHIRE	**SUNNYSIDE,** Langton Gate	2 – 5.30pm
CENTRAL	**KILBRYDE CASTLE,** Dunblane	2 – 5pm
DUMBARTON	**GLENARN,** Rhu	2 – 5.30pm
EAST LOTHIAN	**COLSTOUN,** Haddington	2 – 5pm
EDINBURGH & WEST LOTHIAN	**HETHERSETT,** Balerno	2 – 5.30pm
ISLE OF ARRAN	**STRABANE,** Brodick	2 – 5pm
PERTH & KINROSS	**GLENDOICK,** Perth	2 – 5pm
STEWARTRY OF KIRKCUDBRIGHT	**ROUGHHILLS,** Sandyhills	2 – 5pm
WIGTOWN	**ARDWELL HOUSE GARDENS,** Ardwell	2 – 5pm

TUESDAY 3rd MAY

MIDLOTHIAN .... **GREENFIELD LODGE,** Lasswade   2 – 5pm

THURSDAY 5th MAY

AYRSHIRE .... **CULZEAN CASTLE**
& COUNTRY PARK   10.30am – 5.30pm

SATURDAY & SUNDAY 7th & 8th MAY

ARGYLL .... **ARDUAINE,** Kilmelford   9.30am – 6pm

SUNDAY 8th MAY

DUMBARTON	**ASKIVAL,** Kilcreggan	2 – 5.30pm
EDINBURGH & WEST LOTHIAN	**COLINTON GARDENS,** Edinburgh	2 – 6pm
FIFE	**WHITEHILL,** Aberdour	2 – 5.30pm
PERTH & KINROSS	**BRANKLYN,** Perth	9.30am – sunset
	GLENDOICK, Perth	2 – 5pm
ROSS, CROMARTY, SKYE & INVERNESS	**ALLANGRANGE,** Munlochy	2 – 5.30pm
TWEEDDALE	**DAWYCK BOTANIC GARDEN,** Stobo	10am – 6pm

SATURDAY 14th MAY

ROSS, CROMARTY, SKYE & INVERNESS .... **LOCHALSH WOODLAND**
GARDEN   1 – 5.30pm

SATURDAY & SUNDAY 14th & 15th MAY

ARGYLL	**COLINTRAIVE GARDENS**	2 – 6pm
MIDLOTHIAN	**LASSWADE SPRING GARDENS**	2.30 – 5.30pm

SUNDAY 15th MAY

ANGUS	**BRECHIN CASTLE,** Brechin	2 – 6pm
AYRSHIRE	**ASHCRAIG,** Skelmorlie	2 – 5.30pm
CENTRAL	**TOUCH,** Cambusbarron	2 – 5pm
DUMBARTON	**AUCHENDARROCH,** Tarbet	2 – 5.30pm
DUMFRIES	**CRICHTON ROYAL,** Dumfries	2 – 5pm
EAST LOTHIAN	**LENNOXLOVE,** Haddington	10am – 5pm
EDINBURGH & WEST LOTHIAN	**THE WALLED GARDEN CENTRE,** Hopetoun House	1 – 5pm
FIFE	**BIRKHILL,** Cupar	2.30 – 6pm
	MICKLEGARTH, Aberdour	2 – 5.30pm
MORAY & WEST BANFF	**ALTYRE,** Forres	2 – 6pm
PERTH & KINROSS	**GLENDOICK,** Perth	2 – 5pm
	STOBHALL, by Perth	2 – 6pm
RENFREW, INVERCLYDE & EASTWOOD	**CALDERBANK & CALDERBANK COTTAGE,** Lochwinnoch	2 – 5pm
ROXBURGH	**NEWTON DON,** Kelso	11.30am – 5pm
STEWARTRY OF KIRKCUDBRIGHT	**BARNHOURIE MILL,** Colvend	2 – 5pm
WIGTOWN	**GLENWHAN,** Dunragit	10am – 5pm

WEDNESDAY 18th MAY

CENTRAL .... **NORRIESTON HOUSE,** Thornhill   2 – 5.30pm

SATURDAY 21st MAY

DUMBARTON .... **GEILSTON HOUSE,** Cardross   2 – 5.30pm

SATURDAY & SUNDAY 21st & 22nd MAY

ARGYLL	**ARDKINGLAS HOUSE,** Cairndow	11am – 6pm
	KYLES OF BUTE SMALL GARDENS	2 – 6pm
EDINBURGH & WEST LOTHIAN	**DR NEIL'S GARDEN,** Duddingston	2 – 5pm
PERTH & KINROSS...	**EASTER DUNBARNIE,** Bridge of Earn	2 – 6pm
RENFREW, INVERCLYDE & EASTWOOD......	**RENFREW CENTRAL NURSERY,** Paisley	1 – 5pm

SUNDAY 22nd MAY

ANGUS	**KINNETTLES HOUSE,** Douglastown	2 – 6pm
AYRSHIRE	**AUCHINCRUIVE,** Ayr	1 – 6pm
BERWICKSHIRE	**CHARTERHALL,** Duns	2 – 5pm
DUMBARTON..	**OLD COURT,** Rhu	2 – 5pm
DUMFRIES	**COWHILL TOWER,** Holywood	2 – 5pm
EAST LOTHIAN	**STENTON VILLAGE GARDENS**	2 – 6pm
FIFE	**EARLSHALL CASTLE,** Leuchars	2 – 6pm
LOCHABER, BADENOCH & STRATHSPEY ...	**ACHNACARRY,** Spean Bridge	2 – 5.30pm
PERTH & KINROSS..	**ARDVORLICH,** Lochearnhead	2 – 6pm
	GLENDOICK, Perth	2 – 5pm
	KENNACOIL HOUSE, Dunkeld	2 – 6pm
ROSS, CROMARTY, SKYE & INVERNESS	**LAGGAN HOUSE,** Scaniport	2 – 5pm
STEWARTRY OF KIRKCUDBRIGHT	**DROMINEEN,** Gatehouse of Fleet	2 – 5pm

TUESDAY & WEDNESDAY 24th & 25th MAY

ARGYLL .... **CRINAN HOTEL GARDEN**   10am – 6pm

WEDNESDAY 25th MAY

PERTH & KINROSS... **WESTER DALQUEICH,** Carnbo   2 – 5pm

SATURDAY 28th MAY

ROSS, CROMARTY, SKYE & INVERNESS	**ATTADALE,** Strathcarron	2 – 6pm
	HOUSE OF GRUINARD, by Laide	2 – 6pm

SUNDAY & MONDAY 29th & 30th MAY

CENTRAL .... **DUCHRAY CASTLE,** Aberfoyle   2 – 5pm

SUNDAY 29th MAY

ABERDEEN	**CRICHIE,** Stuartfield	1 – 5pm
	CULQUOICH, Alford	1.30 – 5pm
ANGUS	**CORTACHY CASTLE,** Kirriemuir	2 – 6pm
AYRSHIRE	**DOONHOLM,** Ayr	2 – 5.30pm
BERWICKSHIRE	**MORDINGTON HOUSE,** Paxton	2 – 6pm
	SPRINGHILL, Birgham	2 – 6pm

DUMBARTON	**ROSS PRIORY**, Gartocharn	2 – 6pm
DUMFRIES	**DALSWINTON HOUSE**, Auldgirth	2 – 5pm
EAST LOTHIAN	**TYNINGHAME**, Dunbar	2 – 6pm
ETTRICK & LAUDERDALE	**ALLERLY MAINS AND HOLLYBANK**, Gattonside	2 – 5.30pm
KINCARDINE & DEESIDE	**THE BURN HOUSE & THE BURN GARDEN HOUSE**, Glenesk	2 – 5pm
LOCHABER, BADENOCH & STRATHSPEY	**ARDTORNISH**, Lochaline	2 – 5pm
MIDLOTHIAN	**PENICUIK HOUSE**, Penicuik	2 – 5.30pm
ROSS, CROMARTY, SKYE & INVERNESS	**ALDOURIE CASTLE**, Inverness	2 – 5pm
	NOVAR, Evanton	2 – 6pm
STEWARTRY OF KIRKCUDBRIGHT	**CORSOCK HOUSE**, Castle Douglas	2.30 – 5.30pm
	WALTON PARK, Castle Douglas	2.30 – 5pm
TWEEDDALE	**HAYSTOUN**, Peebles	2 – 5.30pm
WIGTOWN	**LOGAN BOTANIC GARDEN**	10am – 6pm
	LOGAN, Port Logan	10am – 6pm

MONDAY 30th MAY

BERWICKSHIRE	**MANDERSTON**, Duns	2 – 5.30pm
RENFREW, INVERCLYDE & EASTWOOD	**FORMAKIN ESTATE**, Bishopton	11am – 5pm

---

JUNE *For regular openings see pages 10 and 11*

WEDNESDAY 1st JUNE

ROSS, CROMARTY, SKYE & INVERNESS	**TOURNAIG,** Poolewe	2 – 6pm

SATURDAY 4th JUNE

ROSS, CROMARTY, SKYE & INVERNESS	**INVERAN LODGE,** Poolewe	2 – 6pm

SATURDAY & SUNDAY 4th & 5th JUNE

ARGYLL	**COILLE DHARAICH**, Kilmelford	2 – 6pm
	TIGHNAMARA, Kilmelford	2 – 6pm

SUNDAY 5th JUNE

ABERDEEN	**DUNECHT HOUSE GARDENS**	1 – 5pm
	KILDRUMMY CASTLE GARDENS, Alford	10am – 5pm
CENTRAL	**DUNTREATH CASTLE**, Blanefield	2 – 5.30pm
	KILBRYDE CASTLE, Dunblane	2 – 5pm
	PASS HOUSE, Kilmahog	2 – 5.30pm
CLYDESDALE	**NEMPHLAR GARDEN TRAIL**	2 – 5.30pm
DUMBARTON	**THE LINN GARDEN**, Cove	2 – 6pm
EAST LOTHIAN	**HOUSTON MILL**, East Linton	10am – 6pm
EDINBURGH & WEST LOTHIAN	**KIRKNEWTON HOUSE**, Kirknewton	2 – 6pm

FIFE	**FALKLAND PALACE GARDEN**	2 – 5pm
	KIRKLANDS HOUSE, Saline	2 – 5.30pm
LOCHABER, BADENOCH & STRATHSPEY ...	**ARD-DARAICH,** Ardgour	2 – 5pm
PERTH & KINROSS	**BATTLEBY,** Redgorton	2 – 5pm
	MURTHLY CASTLE, by Dunkeld	2 – 6pm
	ROSSIE PRIORY, Inchture	2 – 6pm
ROSS, CROMARTY, SKYE & INVERNESS	**BRAHAN,** Dingwall	2 – 5.30pm
	KYLLACHY, Tomatin	2 – 5.30pm
ROXBURGH	**MERTOUN,** St Boswells	2 – 6pm
STEWARTRY OF KIRKCUDBRIGHT	**HENSOL,** Mossdale	2 – 5pm
TWEEDDALE	**HALLMANOR,** Kirkton Manor	2 – 6pm
WIGTOWN	**WHITEHILLS,** Newton Stewart	2 – 5pm

TUESDAY 7th JUNE

MIDLOTHIAN	**GREENFIELD LODGE,** Lasswade	2 – 5pm

THURSDAY 9th JUNE

EAST LOTHIAN	**SHEPHERD HOUSE,** Inveresk	2 – 5.30pm
ROSS, CROMARTY, SKYE & INVERNESS	**DUNDONNELL,** Little Loch Broom	2 – 5.30pm

FRIDAY & SATURDAY 10th & 11th JUNE

ROSS, CROMARTY, SKYE & INVERNESS	**ACHNASHELLACH STATION HOUSE**	10am – 6pm

SATURDAY & SUNDAY 11th & 12th JUNE

ARGYLL	**ARDENTALLEN GARDENS,** by Lerags	2 – 6pm

SUNDAY 12th JUNE

ABERDEEN	**DUNECHT HOUSE GARDENS**	1 – 5pm
CENTRAL	**NORRIESTON HOUSE,** Thornhill	2 – 5.30pm
	THE BLAIR, Blairlogie	2 – 5pm
DUMBARTON	**WARDS,** Gartocharn	2 – 6pm
DUMFRIES	**SANQUHAR HOUSE,** Sanquhar	2 – 5pm
EDINBURGH & WEST LOTHIAN	**MALLENY HOUSE GARDEN,** Balerno	2 – 5pm
ETTRICK & LAUDERDALE	**CHAPEL-ON-LEADER,** Earlston	2 – 6pm
FIFE	**GILSTON,** Largoward	1.30 – 6pm
	THE MURREL, Aberdour	10am – 5pm
MORAY & WEST BANFF	**DALLAS LODGE,** by Forres	2 – 6pm
PERTH & KINROSS	**BRANKLYN,** Perth	9.30am – sunset
	CLOQUHAT GARDENS, Bridge of Cally	2 – 6pm
	THE BANK HOUSE, Glenfarg	2 – 6pm
ROSS, CROMARTY, SKYE & INVERNESS	**ALLANGRANGE,** Munlochy	2 – 5.30pm
TWEEDDALE	**STOBO WATER GARDEN**	2 – 6pm

WEDNESDAY 15th JUNE
ROSS, CROMARTY, SKYE & INVERNESS .... **DUNDONNELL,** Little Loch Broom   2 – 5.30pm

SATURDAY & SUNDAY 18th & 19th JUNE
EDINBURGH & WEST LOTHIAN .... **ARTHUR LODGE,** Edinburgh   2 – 5pm

SATURDAY 18th JUNE
ROXBURGH.. **TEVIOT WATER GARDEN,** Eckford   6 – 8pm

SUNDAY 19th JUNE
ABERDEEN	**GRANDHOME,** Aberdeen	2.30 – 5.30pm
	HOWEMILL, Craigievar	2 – 6pm
	STATION COTTAGE, Gartly	2 – 5pm
ANGUS	**RESWALLIE,** by Forfar	2 – 5.30pm
AYRSHIRE	**HUGHENDEN,** Troon	2 – 6pm
CLYDESDALE	**LAWHEAD CROFT,** Tarbrax	2 – 6pm
DUMFRIES	**KIRKLAND,** Courance	2 – 5pm
EAST LOTHIAN	**BOWERHOUSE,** Spott	2 – 6pm
ETTRICK & LAUDERDALE	**MIDLEM VILLAGE**	2 – 6pm
FIFE	**BALCASKIE,** Pittenweem	2 – 6pm
	LATHRISK HOUSE & OLD LATHRISK, Freuchie	2 – 5.30pm
RENFREW, INVERCLYDE & EASTWOOD	**DUCHAL,** Kilmacolm	2 – 5pm
ROSS, CROMARTY, SKYE & INVERNESS	**KINKELL CASTLE,** Conon Bridge	2 – 6pm
STEWARTRY OF KIRKCUDBRIGHT	**CALLY GARDENS,** Gatehouse	10am – 5.30pm
WIGTOWN	**BARGALY HOUSE,** Palnure	2 – 5pm

WEDNESDAY 22nd JUNE
CENTRAL .... **NORRIESTON HOUSE,** Thornhill   2 – 5.30pm

SATURDAY 25th JUNE
CAITHNESS & SUTHERLAND .... **DUNROBIN CASTLE & GARDENS,** Golspie   10.30am – 5.30pm

SATURDAY & SUNDAY 25th & 26th JUNE
ARGYLL	**TAYNUILT COTTAGE GARDENS**	2 – 6pm
MIDLOTHIAN	**LASSWADE SUMMER GARDENS**	2 – 5.30pm
TWEEDDALE	**CRINGLETIE HOUSE HOTEL,** Eddleston	2 – 5pm

SUNDAY 26th JUNE
ABERDEEN	**TERTOWIE,** Clinterty	1 – 4pm
ANGUS	**NEWTONMILL,** by Edzell	2 – 5.30pm
AYRSHIRE	**ANNANHILL NURSERY,** Kilmarnock	2 – 5pm
CLYDESDALE	**KITTOCH MILL,** Carmunnock	2 – 5pm
EAST LOTHIAN	**LUFFNESS,** Aberlady	2 – 6pm
FIFE	**KELLIE CASTLE,** Pittenweem	11am – 5pm
	MYRES CASTLE, Auchtermuchty	2 – 5pm
ISLE OF ARRAN	**DOUGARIE**	2 – 6pm
KINCARDINE & DEESIDE	**CRATHES CASTLE,** Banchory	2 – 5pm

MORAY & WEST BANFF	**GORDONSTOUN**, Duffus	2 – 6pm
RENFREW, INVERCLYDE & EASTWOOD	**LUNDERSTON**, Ardgowan	2 – 5pm
ROXBURGH	**BENRIG, BENRIG COTTAGE, MANSFIELD HOUSE & STABLE HOUSE**, St Boswells	2 – 6pm
STEWARTRY OF KIRKCUDBRIGHT	**SOUTHWICK HOUSE**, Dumfries	2 – 5pm

---

JULY   *For regular openings see pages 10 and 11*

SUNDAY 3rd JULY

ANGUS	**BRECHIN CASTLE**, Brechin	2 – 6pm
	GLAMIS CASTLE	10.30am – 5.30pm
AYRSHIRE	**BARNWEIL**, Craigie	2 – 6pm
DUMBARTON	**OLD COURT**, Rhu	2 – 5pm
EAST LOTHIAN	**FORBES LODGE**, Gifford	2 – 6pm
ETTRICK & LAUDERDALE	**LINTHILL**, Lilliesleaf **& SHAWBURN**, Midlem	2 – 5.30pm
FIFE	**HILLSIDE**, Ceres	2 – 5.30pm
	ST ANDREWS BOTANIC GARDEN	10am – 6pm
KINCARDINE & DEESIDE	**BENT**, Laurencekirk	2 – 5pm
STEWARTRY OF KIRKCUDBRIGHT	**BALMACLELLAN HOUSE**, New Galloway	2 – 5pm

TUESDAY 5th JULY

MIDLOTHIAN	**GREENFIELD LODGE**, Lasswade	2 – 5pm

WEDNESDAY 6th JULY

ISLE OF ARRAN	**BRODICK CASTLE & COUNTRY PARK**	10am – 5pm
PERTH & KINROSS	**WESTER DALQUEICH**, Carnbo	2 – 5pm

THURSDAY 7th JULY

ROSS, CROMARTY, SKYE & INVERNESS	**DUNDONNELL**, Little Loch Broom	2 – 5.30pm

SUNDAY 10th JULY

ABERDEEN	**23 DON STREET**, Aberdeen	1.30 – 6pm
ANGUS	**EDZELL VILLAGE**	1.30 – 5.30pm
AYRSHIRE	**SWALLOW HA'**, Symington	2 – 6pm
BERWICKSHIRE	**BUGHTRIG**, Leitholm	2.30 – 5.30pm
CENTRAL	**KILBRYDE CASTLE**, Dunblane	2 – 5pm
	MENTEITH HOUSE, Port of Menteith	2 – 5.30pm
CLYDESDALE	**BIGGAR PARK**, Biggar	2 – 6pm
EAST LOTHIAN	**INVERESK**, near Musselburgh	2 – 6pm
EDINBURGH & WEST LOTHIAN	**PHILPSTOUN HOUSE**, Linlithgow	2 – 5.30pm
FIFE	**HILL OF TARVIT**, Cupar	11am – 5pm
KINCARDINE & DEESIDE	**DRUM CASTLE**, Drumoak	2 – 5pm
PERTH & KINROSS	**DUNBARNEY HOUSE**, Bridge of Earn	2 – 6pm

ROSS, CROMARTY, SKYE & INVERNESS .... **ALLANGRANGE,** Munlochy   2 – 5.30pm
ROXBURGH .... **CORBET TOWER,** Morebattle   2 – 6pm

WEDNESDAY 13th JULY

CENTRAL .... **NORRIESTON HOUSE,** Thornhill   2 – 5.30pm
ROSS, CROMARTY, SKYE & INVERNESS .... **DUNDONNELL,** Little Loch Broom   2 – 5.30pm

SUNDAY 17th JULY

BERWICKSHIRE .... **NETHERBYRES,** Eyemouth   2 – 6pm
CLYDESDALE .... **LAWHEAD CROFT,** Tarbrax   2 – 6pm
ETTRICK & LAUDERDALE .... **MELLERSTAIN,** Gordon   12.30 – 6.30pm
KINCARDINE & DEESIDE .... **ARBUTHNOTT HOUSE,** Laurencekirk   2 – 5pm
     BOGARN & HOUSE OF STRACHAN   2 – 5pm
ROXBURGH .... **MONTEVIOT,** Jedburgh   2 – 5pm
STEWARTRY OF KIRKCUDBRIGHT .... **ARGRENNAN HOUSE,** Castle Douglas   2 – 5pm

WEDNESDAY 20th JULY

AYRSHIRE .... **CULZEAN CASTLE &**
     COUNTRY PARK   10.30am – 5.30pm
CAITHNESS & SUTHERLAND .... **CASTLE OF MEY**   2 – 6pm
ROSS, CROMARTY, SKYE & INVERNESS .... **HOUSE OF GRUINARD,** Laide   2 – 6pm

SATURDAY 23rd JULY

ROSS, CROMARTY, SKYE & INVERNESS .... **LOCHALSH WOODLAND GARDEN**   1 – 5.30pm

SATURDAY & SUNDAY 23rd & 24th JULY

FIFE .... **CRAIL GARDENS**   2 – 6pm

SUNDAY 24th JULY

ABERDEEN .... **BYTH HOUSE,** New Byth   2 – 5pm
     LEITH HALL, Kennethmont   2 – 6pm
ARGYLL .... **ARDCHATTAN PRIORY FETE**
AYRSHIRE .... **CARNELL,** Hurlford   2 – 5pm
CENTRAL .... **CAMBUSMORE,** Callander   2 – 5.30pm
CLYDESDALE .... **THE OLD MANSE,** Elsrickle   2 – 6pm
FIFE .... **HILTON HOUSE,** Cupar   2.30 – 5.30pm
KINCARDINE & DEESIDE .... **DOUNESIDE HOUSE,** Tarland   2 – 6pm
     GLENBERVIE HOUSE, Drumlithie   2 – 5pm
PERTH & KINROSS .... **BORELAND,** Killin   2 – 5.30pm
STEWARTRY OF KIRKCUDBRIGHT .... **SPOTTES,** Haugh-of-Urr   2 – 5pm
TWEEDDALE .... **PORTMORE,** Eddleston   2 – 5pm
     QUARTER HOUSE, Broughton   2 – 6pm

THURSDAY 28TH JULY

CAITHNESS & SUTHERLAND .... **CASTLE OF MEY**   2 – 6pm

SATURDAY 30th JULY

CAITHNESS & SUTHERLAND .... **HOUSE OF TONGUE**   2 – 6pm

SUNDAY 31st JULY

ABERDEEN	**BEECHGROVE GARDEN**	11am – 5pm
	CASTLE FRASER, Kemnay	2 – 5pm
CLYDESDALE	**BAITLAWS,** Lamington	2 – 6pm
	GLENBRECK, Coulter	2 – 6pm
KINCARDINE & DEESIDE	**BALMANNO,** Marykirk	2 – 5.30pm
RENFREW, INVERCLYDE & EASTWOOD	**GREENBANK GARDEN,** Clarkston	2 – 5pm
ROSS, CROMARTY, SKYE & INVERNESS	**INVEREWE,** Poolewe	9.30am – sunset

AUGUST *For regular openings see pages 10 and 11*

TUESDAY 2nd AUGUST

MIDLOTHIAN	**GREENFIELD LODGE,** Lasswade	2 – 5pm

WEDNESDAY 3rd AUGUST

ISLE OF ARRAN	**BRODICK CASTLE & COUNTRY PARK**	10am – 5pm
PERTH & KINROSS	**WESTER DALQUEICH,** Carnbo	2 – 5pm
ROSS, CROMARTY, SKYE & INVERNESS	**TOURNAIG,** Poolewe	2 – 6pm

SATURDAY 6th AUGUST

AYRSHIRE	**BARR VILLAGE GARDENS**	1 – 5pm
CAITHNESS & SUTHERLAND	**SANDSIDE HOUSE GARDENS,** by Reay	2.30pm

SUNDAY 7th AUGUST

ABERDEEN	**HADDO HOUSE,** Tarves	2 – 5pm
	PITMEDDEN GARDENS	2 – 5pm
ANGUS	**NEWTYLE VILLAGE & KINPURNIE CASTLE**	2 – 6pm
AYRSHIRE	**SKELDON,** Dalrymple	2 – 6pm
CAITHNESS & SUTHERLAND	**LANGWELL,** Berriedale	2 – 6pm
CLYDESDALE	**CULTER ALLERS,** Coulter	2 – 6pm
	SIX FATHOMS, Eaglesham	2 – 5pm
EDINBURGH & WEST LOTHIAN	**SUNTRAP,** Gogarbank	2.30 – 5pm
ETTRICK & LAUDERDALE	**ABBOTSFORD,** Melrose	2 – 5.30pm
FIFE	**FALKLAND PALACE GARDEN**	2 – 5pm
	MICKLEGARTH, Aberdour	2 – 5.30pm
PERTH & KINROSS	**CLUNIEMORE,** Pitlochry	2 – 5.30pm
	DRUMMOND CASTLE GARDENS, Muthill	2 – 6pm
ROSS, CROMARTY, SKYE & INVERNESS	**SCATWELL,** Muir of Ord	2 – 6pm
ROXBURGH	**YETHOLM VILLAGE GARDENS**	2 – 6pm
STEWARTRY OF KIRKCUDBRIGHT	**THREAVE SCHOOL OF GARDENING,** Castle Douglas	9am – 5.30pm

SATURDAY & SUNDAY 13th & 14th AUGUST

CENTRAL .... **ORCHARDLEA HOUSE,** Callander   2 – 5.30pm
FIFE .... **PITTENWEEM GARDENS**   2 – 5.30pm

SUNDAY 14th AUGUST

AYRSHIRE .... **BLAIRQUHAN,** Straiton   1.30 – 4.30pm
CAITHNESS & SUTHERLAND .... **LANGWELL,** Berriedale   2 – 6pm
CENTRAL .... **KILBRYDE CASTLE,** Dunblane   2 – 5pm
EDINBURGH & WEST LOTHIAN .... **SOUTH QUEENSFERRY & DALMENY**   2 – 6pm
PERTH & KINROSS .... **MEGGINCH CASTLE,** Errol   2 – 5pm
STEWARTRY OF KIRKCUDBRIGHT .... **CALLY GARDENS,** Gatehouse   10am – 5.30pm

SATURDAY 20th AUGUST

CLYDESDALE .... **17 DOUGALSTON AVENUE,** Milngavie   2 – 5pm

SATURDAY & SUNDAY 20th & 21st AUGUST

EDINBURGH & WEST LOTHIAN .... **DR NEIL'S GARDEN,** Duddingston   2 – 5pm

SUNDAY 21st AUGUST

ABERDEEN .... **ESSLEMONT,** Ellon   1.30 – 5pm
AYRSHIRE .... **LAGG HOUSE,** Dunure   2 – 5pm
CAITHNESS & SUTHERLAND .... **DUNBEATH CASTLE**   2 – 6pm
EDINBURGH & WEST LOTHIAN .... **BELGRAVE CRESCENT GARDENS**   2 – 5pm

SUNDAY 28th AUGUST

ABERDEEN .... **DUNECHT HOUSE GARDENS**   1 – 5pm
TILLYPRONIE, Tarland   2 – 5pm
MORAY & WEST BANFF .... **RELUGAS HOUSE,** by Forres   2 – 6pm

MONDAY 29th AUGUST

BERWICKSHIRE .... **MANDERSTON,** Duns   2 – 5.30pm

---

SEPTEMBER   *For regular openings see pages 10 and 11*

FRIDAY 2nd SEPTEMBER

CAITHNESS & SUTHERLAND .... **CASTLE OF MEY**   2 – 6pm

SUNDAY 4th SEPTEMBER

DUMBARTON .... **THE HILL HOUSE,** Helensburgh
Plant Sale   11am – 5pm

TUESDAY 6th SEPTEMBER

MIDLOTHIAN .... **GREENFIELD LODGE,** Lasswade   2 – 5pm

SUNDAY 11th SEPTEMBER

CENTRAL .... **KILBRYDE CASTLE,** Dunblane   2 – 5pm
FIFE .... **THE MURREL,** Aberdour   10am – 5pm

SUNDAY 18th SEPTEMBER

FIFE .... **THE MURREL,** Aberdour   10am – 5pm

SUNDAY 25th SEPTEMBER

LOCHABER, BADENOCH & STRATHSPEY ... **ABERARDER,** Kinlochlaggan   2.30 – 5.30pm
                                             ARDVERIKIE, Kinlochlaggan   2.30 – 5.30pm

---

OCTOBER   *For regular openings see pages 10 and 11*

SATURDAY & SUNDAY 1st & 2nd OCTOBER

FIFE .... **HILL OF TARVIT PLANT SALE**
                                   Saturday: 10.30am – 4pm
                                   Sunday: 2 – 5pm

SUNDAY 9th OCTOBER

CENTRAL .... **KILBRYDE CASTLE,** Dunblane   2 – 5pm

ABERDEEN
(GRAMPIAN REGION)

Joint District Organisers:	**Mrs Wolrige Gordon of Esslemont,** Esslemont House, Ellon, AB41 8PA
	Mrs M Dingwall Fordyce, West Affleck, Maud, Peterhead AB42 8RN
Area Organisers:	**Mrs D H W Brown,** Glenbogie, Lumsden AB54 4JA
	Mrs W Bruce, Logie House, Ellon AB41 8LH
	Mrs G F Collie, Morkeu, Cults AB1 9PT
	Mrs F G Lawson, Asloun, Alford AB33 8NR
	Mrs A Robertson, Drumblade House, Huntly AB54 6ER
Hon. Treasurer:	**Mrs M Stewart-Richardson,** Manse of Glenbuchat, Strathdon AB36 8TN

DATES OF OPENING

23 Don Street, Old Aberdeen	Daily April – October by appt.	
Kildrummy Castle Gardens.	Daily April – October	
Pitmedden Garden	Daily May – September 10am – 5.30pm	
Auchmacoy, Ellon	Sunday 17 April	1.30 – 4.30pm
Crichie, Stuartfield	Sunday 29 May	1 – 5pm
Culquoich, Alford	Sunday 29 May	1.30 – 5pm
Dunecht House Garden, Dunecht	Sunday 5 June	1 – 5pm
Kildrummy Castle Gardens, Alford	Sunday 5 June	10am – 5pm
Dunecht House Garden, Dunecht	Sunday 12 June	1 – 5pm
Grandhome, Aberdeen	Sunday 19 June	2.30 – 5.30pm
Howemill, Craigievar, Alford	Sunday 19 June	2 – 6pm
Station Cottage, Gartly	Sunday 19 June	2 – 5pm
Tertowie Garden, Clinterty	Sunday 26 June	1 – 4pm
23 Don Street, Old Aberdeen	Sunday 10 July	1.30 – 6pm
Byth House, New Byth, Turriff	Sunday 24 July	2 – 5pm
Leith Hall, Kennethmont, by Huntly	Sunday 24 July	2 – 6pm
Beechgrove Garden.	Sunday 31 July	11am – 5pm
Castle Fraser, Kemnay	Sunday 31 July	2 – 5pm
Haddo House, Tarves	Sunday 7 August	2 – 5pm
Pitmedden Gardens, Pitmedden	Sunday 7 August	2 – 5pm
Esslemont, Ellon	Sunday 21 August	1.30 – 5pm
Dunecht House Gardens, Dunecht	Sunday 28 August	1 – 5pm
Tillypronie, Tarland	Sunday 28 August	2 – 5pm

23 DON STREET, Old Aberdeen ♿
(Miss M Mackechnie)
A secret small walled garden in historic Old Aberdeen. Recently developed using existing features giving a long established atmosphere. Wide range of unusual plants and old-fashioned roses. Small pool with fish and aquatic plants. Park at St Machar Cathedral, short walk down Chanonry to Don Street, turn right. City plan ref: P7.
Admission 80p Children 40p OAPs 50p
OPEN APRIL TO OCTOBER BY APPOINTMENT Tel: 0224 487269.
SUNDAY 10th JULY 1.30 – 6pm
40% to Cat Protection League

AUCHMACOY, Ellon ♿
(Captain D W S Buchan)
Auchmacoy House policies feature an attractive display of tens of thousands of daffodils. Teas.
Admission £1.00 Children & OAPs 50p
SUNDAY 17th APRIL 1.30 – 4.30 pm
40% to Gordon Highlanders Museum Appeal

BEECHGROVE GARDEN, Aberdeen ♿
(BBC Scotland)
BBC Scotland's television gardeners will be in attendance. NO CARS. 1½ miles from Aberdeen city centre. City bus nos. 13 & 22.
Admission £1.00 Children & OAPs 50p
SUNDAY 31st JULY 11 am – 5 pm. Disabled from 10.30 am
All proceeds to Scotland's Gardens Scheme

 # BYTH HOUSE, New Byth, Turriff ♿ partially
(Col R Windsor & Mr & Mrs A Windsor)
Herbaceous and shrub borders, herb gardens, kitchen garden. Woodland walk. Pony rides. Teas. Plant stall. New Byth is off A98.
Admission £1.00 Children & OAPs 50p
SUNDAY 24th JULY 2 – 5 pm
40% to Riding for the Disabled (Banff & Buchan branch)

CASTLE FRASER, Kemnay ♿
(The National Trust for Scotland)
Castle Fraser, one of the most spectacular of the Castles of Mar, belongs to the same period of native architectural achievements as Crathes Castle and Craigievar Castle. The walled garden has been fully restored by the Trust and forms a delightful adjunct to the Castle. Plant sales. Tea room. Trails, pipe band, stalls, competitions, rides. Near Kemnay, off B993.
Admission £1.00 Children & OAPs 50p
SUNDAY 31st JULY 2 – 5 pm
40% to NTS Threave Bursary Fund
For other opening details see page 141

CRICHIE, Stuartfield   ♿   (in part)
(Mr & Mrs G S Burnett-Stuart)
Mature woodland garden with collection of flowering shrubs, azaleas and rhododendrons. Light refreshments. Walks. Plant stall. Turn left off A92. Nine miles north of Ellon and west of Peterhead. Signposted Stuartfield 1½ miles.
Admission £1.50 Children & OAPs 50p
SUNDAY 29th MAY 1 – 5 pm
40% to St Drostan's Church, Old Deer

CULQUOICH, Alford
(Mr & Mrs A J S Bell Tawse)
Natural woodlands, including an interesting pinetum, shrubs, spring bulbs, azaleas and rhododendrons. Tea and biscuits. Garden is west of Glenkindie village, opposite Glenkindie House, off main Alford-Strathdon road, A97.
Admission £1.00 Children & OAPs 50p
SUNDAY 29th MAY 1.30 – 5 pm
40% to Arthritis and Rheumatism Council

DUNECHT HOUSE GARDENS, Dunecht ♿ (partly)
(Viscount Cowdray)
Romanesque addition, 1877, by G Edmund Street, to original House by John & William Smith. Herbaceous borders, heath and wild garden. Light refreshments. Cars free. Dunecht 1 mile. Routes A974, A944, B 977.
Admission £1.50 Children 50p
SUNDAY 5th and SUNDAY 12th JUNE 1 – 5 pm
40% to Queen's Nursing Institute (Scotland)
SUNDAY 28th AUGUST 1 – 5 pm
40% to Aberdeen Branch Riding for the Disabled

ESSLEMONT, Ellon ♿
(Captain & Mrs Wolrige Gordon)
Victorian house set in wooded policies above River Ythan. Roses and shrubs in garden with double yew hedges (17th and 18th centuries). Music, plant stalls, charity stalls. Teas. Ellon 2 miles. Take A920 from Ellon-Oldmeldrum/Pitmedden road.
Admission £1.00 Children 50p
SUNDAY 21st AUGUST 1.30 – 5 pm
20% to Epilepsy Association of Scotland
20% between Ellon & Tarves Boys' Brigade and St Mary on the Rock Graveyard.

GRANDHOME, Aberdeen ♿
(Mr & Mrs D R Paton)
18th century walled garden, incorporating rose garden; policies with rhododendrons, azaleas, mature trees and shrubs. Plant stall. Teas. Sorry no dogs. On River Don 2 miles north west of north side of Persley Bridge, or, from Aberdeen via Persley Bridge, turn left at Danestone roundabout.
Admission £1.00 Children & OAPs 50p
SUNDAY 19th JUNE 2.30 – 5.30 pm
20% to Royal Society for the Prevention of Cruelty to Children
20% to Epilepsy Association of Scotland

HADDO HOUSE, Tarves ♿
(The National Trust for Scotland)
Attractive and prolific rose garden. Good herbaceous borders. Teas. House tour. Off B999
4 miles north of Pitmedden, 19 miles north of Aberdeen.
Admission £1.00 Children & OAPs 50p
SUNDAY 7th AUGUST 2 – 5 pm
40% to NTS Threave Bursary Fund
For details of other openings see page 141

HOWEMILL, Craigievar
(Mr D Atkinson)
Young garden with a wide range of unusual alpines, shrubs and herbaceous plants. Plant
stall. Teas. From Alford take A980 Alford/Lumphanan road. Suitable for disabled with
help. No dogs please.
Admission £1.00 Children under 12 free
SUNDAY 19th JUNE 2 – 6 pm
40% to Cancer Relief Macmillan Fund

KILDRUMMY CASTLE GARDENS, Alford ♿ (with help)
(Kildrummy Garden Trust)
April shows the gold of the lysichitons in the water garden, and the small bulbs
naturalised beside the copy of the 14th century Brig o' Balgownie. Rhododendrons and
azaleas from April (frost permitting). September/October brings colchicums and brilliant
colour with acers, fothergillas and viburnums. Plants for sale. Play area. Video room.
Nature table in spring. Wheelchair facilities. Car park free inside hotel main entrance.
Coach park up hotel delivery entrance. Parties by arrangement. Tel: 09755 71277/71203.
Kildrummy on A97, 10 miles from Alford, 17 miles from Huntly.
Admission £1.70 Children 6 – 16 50p
Open daily APRIL – OCTOBER
SUNDAY 5th JUNE 10 am – 5 pm
20% to Queen's Nursing Institute (Scotland) and
20% to the Gardens Fund of the National Trust for Scotland

LEITH HALL, Kennethmont
(The National Trust for Scotland)
Quadrangular harled mansion dating from 1650. Home of Leith and Leith-Hay family
until 1945. Public rooms contain interesting furniture, personal possessions and
mementoes. The house tour incorporates all of the first floor, including the splendid oval
room and a military collection on second floor. Garden contains a rock garden and zig-
zag herbaceous and catmint borders. Chinese moon gate and Pictish stones. Extensive
grounds with 18th century stables, ponds, including one with a bird observation hide,
three countryside walks with one to a viewpoint overlooking surrounding countryside.
Admission to house £3.50, children £1.80. Teas. Pipe band, family games, boat rides,
stalls, competitions. On B9002 near Kennethmont.
Admission £1.00 Children & OAPs 50p
SUNDAY 24th JULY 2 – 6 pm
40% to NTS Threave Bursary Fund
For details of other openings see page 138

PITMEDDEN GARDEN, Ellon   ♿
(The National Trust for Scotland)
Garden created by Lord Pitmedden in 1675. Recreated by the Trust from 1952, and is one of the very few gardens of this period in Scotland. Elaborate floral designs in parterres of box edging. Herbaceous borders, yew buttresses, pavilions, fountains and sundials. Also Museum of Farming Life, Visitor Centre, woodland walk. Special rates for pre-booked coach parties.
Admission £3.00 Children & OAPs £1.50
Open daily 1st MAY to 30th SEPTEMBER 10 am – 5.30 pm (Last entry 5 pm)
SUNDAY 7th AUGUST 2 – 5 pm
40% to NTS Threave Bursary Fund
For details of other openings see page 139

STATION COTTAGE, Gartly
(Travers & Betty Cosgrove)
Century old quarry converted into a "secret garden" by generations of railwaymen. Old cottage plants. Climbing pathways through wild garden. Railway site preserved. Teas by the Parish of Noth. Plant stall. Railway still in use. 5 miles south of Huntly on A97 towards Rhynie. Follow signs for Gartly from A96.
Admission £1.00 Children & OAPs 50p
SUNDAY 19th JUNE 2 – 5 pm
40% to Parish of Noth, Church of Scotland

TERTOWIE, Clinterty   ♿
(Aberdeen College)
Half-acre walled garden with herbaceous and mixed borders, bulbs and climbers. Four acres of grounds set in mature woodland with shade garden, peat garden, bog garden, rose garden. Small garden for the disabled. National Rubus Collection. Plant stall. Teas. Woodland walks through surrounding area. Follow signs for Clinterty from A96 Aberdeen/Inverness road, Tertowie signposted at next junction. From A944 Aberdeen/Alford road, signposted just after 5 Mile garage. Gardens open by kind permission of Aberdeen College. Dogs on lead, please.
Admission £1.00 Children & OAPs 50p
SUNDAY 26th JUNE 1 – 4 pm
40% to Aberdeen & North East Council of Disability

TILLYPRONIE, Tarland   ♿
(The Hon Philip Astor)
Late Victorian house. Herbaceous borders, terraced garden with pond at bottom. Shrubs, heaths and ornamental trees in pinetum. Vegetable garden. Superb views. Picnic area. Free car park. Dogs on lead, please. Teas.
Admission £1.00 Children 50p
SUNDAY 28th AUGUST 2 – 5 pm
All proceeds to Scotland's Gardens Scheme

ANGUS
(TAYSIDE REGION)

District Organiser: **Mrs Jonathan Stansfeld,** Dunninald, By Montrose DD10 9TD

Area Organisers: **Miss Ruth Dundas,** Caddam, Kinnordy, Kirriemuir DD8 4LP
Mrs R Ephraums, Damside, Leysmill, Arbroath DD11 4RS
Mrs R H V Learoyd, Priestoun, Edzell DD9 7UD
Mrs T D Lloyd-Jones, Reswallie House, by Forfar DD8 2SA
Mrs M Spencer, Airlie Castle, Kirriemuir DD8 5NG

Hon. Treasurer: **Col R H B Learoyd,** Priestoun, Edzell DD9 7UD

DATES OF OPENING

House of Pitmuies, Guthrie, by Forfar .... Daily 1 April – 31 Oct 10am – 5pm

Brechin Castle, Brechin	Sunday 15 May	2 – 6pm
Kinnettles House, by Forfar	Sunday 22 May	2 – 6pm
Cortachy Castle, Kirriemuir	Sunday 29 May	2 – 6pm
Reswallie, by Forfar.	Sunday 19 June	2 – 5.30pm
Newtonmill, by Edzell	Sunday 26 June	2 – 5.30 pm
Brechin Castle, Brechin	Sunday 3 July	2 – 6pm
Glamis Castle.	Sunday 3 July	10.30am – 5.30pm
Edzell Village.	Sunday 10 July	1.30 – 5.30pm
Newtyle village & Kinpurnie Castle.	Sunday 7 August	2 – 6pm

BRECHIN CASTLE, Brechin

(The Earl & Countess of Dalhousie)

Ancient fortress of Scottish kings on cliff overlooking River Southesk. Rebuilt by Alexander Edward – completed in 1711. Extensive walled garden half a mile from Castle with ancient and new plantings and mown lawn approach. Rhododendrons, azaleas, bulbs, interesting trees, wild garden. Tea in garden. Car parking free. Brechin 1 mile. Route A94.

Admission £1.00 Children 50p

SUNDAY 15th MAY and SUNDAY 3rd July 2 – 6 pm

15% to RSSPCC, 15% to Save the Children Fund, 10% to NCCPG

CORTACHY CASTLE, Kirriemuir

(The Earl & Countess of Airlie)

16th century castellated house. Additions in 1872 by David Bryce. Spring garden and wild pond garden with azaleas, primroses and rhododendrons. Garden of fine American specie trees and river walk along South Esk. Teas. Garden quiz. Kirriemuir 5 miles. Route B955.

Admission £1.75 Children 25p

SUNDAY 29th MAY 2 – 6 pm

40% to Scout Association of Scotland

EDZELL VILLAGE

Walk round 12 or 13 gardens in Edzell village. Edzell Castle is also on view. Teas extra. Tickets are on sale in the village and a plan is issued with the tickets. Pipe band. Plant stall.

Admission £1.00 Children 20p

SUNDAY 10th JULY 1.30 – 5.30 pm

40% to Angus Talking Newspaper for the Blind

GLAMIS CASTLE, Glamis

(The Earl & Countess of Strathmore & Kinghorne)

Family home of the Earls of Strathmore and a Royal residence since 1372. Childhood home of HM Queen Elizabeth the Queen Mother, birthplace of HRH the Princess Margaret, and legendary setting for Shakespeare's play "Macbeth". Five-storey L-shaped tower block dating from 15th century, remodelled 1606, containing magnificent rooms with wide range of historic pictures, furniture, porcelain, etc. Spacious grounds with river and woodland paths. Nature trail. Impressive policy timbers. Formal garden. Restaurant. Glamis 1 mile A94.

Admission to Castle and grounds: £4.20, OAPs £3.30, Children £2.30.

Admission: Grounds only £2.00 Children & OAPs £1.00

SUNDAY 3rd JULY 10.30 am – 5.30 pm

40% to Save the Children Fund

HOUSE OF PITMUIES, Guthrie, by Forfar

(Mrs Farquhar Ogilvie)

Semi-formal old walled gardens adjoining 18th century house. Massed spring bulbs, roses, herbaceous borders and a wide variety of shrubs. Old fashioned roses in summer with long borders of herbaceous perennials and superb delphiniums. Riverside walk with fine trees, interesting turreted doocot and "Gothic" wash-house. Dogs on lead please. Rare and unusual plants for sale. Fruit in season. Friockheim 1½ miles. Route A932.

Admission £1.50

Daily 1st APRIL to 31st OCTOBER 10 am – 5 pm

Donation to Scotland's Gardens Scheme

KINNETTLES HOUSE, Douglastown, by Forfar
(Mr & Mrs Hugh Walker-Munro)
Rhododendron walk and rare trees. Formal terraced garden. Three miles south of Forfar on A94. Teas. Signed from main road or Dundee/Forfar road, 8 miles. Follow signs for Douglastown.
Admission £1.50 Children free
SUNDAY 22nd MAY 2 – 6 pm
40% to Kirriemuir Day Centre

KINPURNIE CASTLE, Newtyle
(Sir James Cayzer)
Early 20th century house (not open). Panoramic views of the vale of Strathmore and the Grampians. Shrubs and herbaceous garden. Teas at Newtyle Village Hall. Admission price includes both gardens. Free parking. Route B954. Dundee 10 miles, Perth 18 miles. JOINT OPENING WITH NEWTYLE VILLAGE GARDENS
Admission £1.50 Children 25p
SUNDAY 7th AUGUST 2 – 6 pm
40% to Angus branch, British Red Cross

 # NEWTONMILL, by Edzell   &

(Mr & Mrs Rickman)
A walled garden comprising of herbaceous borders, rose and peony beds and vegetable beds. Formal layout with view to house. Donkey rides. Hoopla stall. Plant stall. No dogs please. Teas. B966 Brechin/Edzell road.
Admission £1.50 Children 50p
SUNDAY 26th JUNE 2 – 5.30 pm
40% to The Scottish Dyslexia Trust

NEWTYLE VILLAGE   & (with assistance)
Several cottage gardens, planted in a variety of styles, may be visited in the course of a short walk round the village of Newtyle. The village, with its regular street plan, was laid out in 1832 next to the northern terminus of Scotland's first passenger railway. Tickets and plan on sale in the village. Plants for sale. Teas in Village Hall. Admission price includes both gardens. Newtyle is on B954 between Meigle and Dundee, 2 miles off A94 between Coupar Angus and Glamis. JOINT OPENING WITH KINPURNIE CASTLE
Admission £1.50 Children 25p
SUNDAY 7th AUGUST 2 – 6 pm
40% to Angus branch, British Red Cross

RESWALLIE, by Forfar
(Col & Mrs T D Lloyd-Jones)
18th century house set in policies of 120 acres. Woodland walks with many interesting trees. Walled herbaceous garden. Vintage cars and motor cycles on display. Plant stall. Teas. Free car parking. Off A932 Forfar/Friockheim road. Reswallie signposted to the left.
Admission £1.50 Children 50p
SUNDAY 19th JUNE 2 – 5.30 pm
40% to British Red Cross Society

ARGYLL
(STRATHCLYDE REGION)

District Organiser:	**Lt Cmdr H D Campbell-Gibson,** Tighnamara, Melfort, Kilmelford PA34 4XD
Area Organisers:	**Mr Frank Airey,** Tigh-na-mara, Tighnabruaich PA21 2EB
	Miss Diana Crosland, Maam, Glen Shira, Inveraray PA32 8XH
	Mrs Michael Reynolds, Ardachy, Connel, By Oban PA37 1RF
Hon. Treasurer:	**Lt Cmdr H D Campbell-Gibson**

DATES OF OPENING

Achnacloich, Connel .... Daily 3 April – 26 June and
2 August – 31 October   10am – 6pm

An Cala, Ellenabeich .... Daily 9 March – 30 September   10am – 6pm

Ardchattan Priory, North Connel .... Daily 1 April – 30 October   9am – 9pm

Ardkinglas Woodland Garden................. Open all year

Ardmaddy Castle, Balvicar .... Daily 15 March – 31 October

Barguillean's 'Angus Garden' Taynuilt .. Open all year

Coille Dharaich, Kilmelford .... By appointment

Crarae Glen Garden, Minard .... Daily April-October   9am – 6pm
Winter during daylight hours

Dalnaheish, Tayvallich .... April-October by appointment

Druimavuic House, Appin .... Daily 17 April – 2 July   10am – 6pm

Druimneil House, Port Appin .... Daily 28 March – 19 June   9am – 6pm

Glenfeochan House Hotel, Kilmore .... Daily 15 March – 31 October   10am – 6pm

Jura House, Ardfin, Isle of Jura .... Open all year   9am – 5pm

Kinlochlaich House Gardens, Appin ...... Open all year   9.30am – 5.30pm or dusk
(except Suns. mid Oct-Mar)

Tighnamara, Kilmelford .... By appointment, Spring-Autumn

Torosay Castle Gardens............................. Open all year
Summer: 9am – 7pm   Winter: Sunrise-Sunset

Arduaine, Kilmelford	Sat & Sun 7/8 May	9.30 – 6pm
Colintraive Gardens Weekend.............................	Sat & Sun 14/15 May	2 – 6pm
Ardkinglas House, Cairndow	Sat & Sun 21/22 May	11am – 6pm
Kyles of Bute Gardens	Sat & Sun 21/22 May	2 – 6pm
Crinan Hotel Garden	Tue & Wed 24/25 May	10am – 6pm
Coille Dharaich, Kilmelford	Sat & Sun 4/5 June	2 – 6pm
Tighnamara, Kilmelford	Sat & Sun 4/5 June	2 – 6pm
Ardentallen Gardens, Lerags	Sat & Sun 11/12 June	2 – 6pm
Taynuilt Cottage Gardens	Sat & Sun 25/26 June	2 – 6pm
Ardchattan Priory Fete	Sunday 24 July	

ACHNACLOICH, Connel &

(Mrs T E Nelson)

Scottish baronial house by John Starforth of Glasgow. Succession of bulbs, flowering shrubs, rhododendrons, azaleas and primulas. Woodland garden above Loch Etive. Plants for sale. Admission by collecting box. 3 miles east of Connel.

Admission £1.00 Children free OAPs 50p

Daily from 3rd APRIL to 26th JUNE & 2nd AUGUST to 31st OCTOBER 10 am – 6 pm

40% between Queen's Nursing Institute (Scotland) and the Gardens Fund of the National Trust for Scotland

AN CALA, Ellenabeich, Isle of Seil

(Mr & Mrs Thomas Downie)

A small garden of under five acres designed in the 1930s, An Cala sits snugly in its horse-shoe shelter of surrounding cliffs. A very pretty garden with streams, waterfall, ponds, many herbaceous plants as well as azaleas, rhododendrons and cherry trees in spring. Proceed south from Oban on Campbeltown road for eight miles, turn right at Easdale sign, a further eight miles along B844; garden between school and Inshaig Park Hotel.

Admission £1.00 Children free

Daily from 9th MARCH to 30th SEPTEMBER 10 am – 6 pm

Donation to Scotland's Gardens Scheme

ARDCHATTAN PRIORY, North Connel &

(Lt Col R Campbell-Preston)

Beautifully situated on the north side of Loch Etive. The Priory founded in 1230 was the scene of the last Gaelic Parliament. The second oldest inhabited house in Scotland. Formal garden in front of house with two herbaceous, three shrub and a rose border. Wild garden west of house with azaleas, shrub roses, 30 varieties of sorbus and many other shrubs and trees. The front garden leads down to Loch Etive with beautiful views east and west. Tea and light lunches provided daily from 1st April to 30th September. Plant stall. Oban 10 miles. From north turn left off A828 at Barcaldine (11 miles south of Appin) on B845 for 6 miles. From Oban or the east on A85, cross Connel Bridge and turn first right. Proceed east on Bonawe road.

Admission £1.00 Children free

Daily from 1st APRIL to 30th OCTOBER 9 am – 9 pm

Donation to Scotland's Gardens Scheme

A fête will be held on **SUNDAY 24th JULY** when the House and Garden will be open.

ARDENTALLEN GARDENS, Lerags, by Oban &

ARDENTALLEN HOUSE (Mrs B K Stein)

Small wild garden with rhododendrons, azaleas and heathers.

SONAS (Mr & Mrs C S Motley)

Small garden created in the 1960s from an old quarry. Trees, shrubs, primulas, herbaceous, heathers and rockery. Teas. Home Baking. Take sign to Lerags about one mile south of Oban on A816 until right turn "Private road to Lower Ardentallen". Signposted from there.

Admission £1.00 includes both gardens. Accompanied children free

SATURDAY & SUNDAY 11th & 12th JUNE 2 – 6 pm

20% to Cancer Relief Macmillan Fund 20% to Alzheimer's Society, Oban

ARDKINGLAS HOUSE, Cairndow   ♿
(Mr S J Noble)

Set around Ardkinglas House, Robert Lorimer's favourite work, the informal garden of around five acres contains magnificent azaleas, trees and other shrubs. The "Caspian", a large pool, enhances the garden's beauty. Teas, coffee, soft drinks and home baking. Plant stall. Adjacent to Ardkinglas Woodland Gardens. Turn into Cairndow village from A83 Glasgow-Campbeltown road. Enter Ardkinglas estate through iron gates.

Admission £1.00 Children free OAPs 50p

SATURDAY & SUNDAY 21st & 22nd MAY 11 am – 6 pm

40% to Ardkinglas Arts Trust

ARDKINGLAS WOODLAND GARDEN, Cairndow   ♿ (partly)
(Ardkinglas Estate)

Large selection of rhododendrons, azaleas and spring flowering shrubs. Famous collection of conifers including Britain's tallest tree and "Europe's mightiest conifer". Free car park. Dogs allowed on lead. Entrance through Cairndow village off A83.

Admission £1.00

OPEN DAILY ALL YEAR ROUND

Donation to Scotland's Gardens Scheme

ARDMADDY CASTLE, Balvicar, by Oban   ♿ (mostly)
(Mr & Mrs Charles Struthers)

Ardmaddy Castle, with its woodlands and walled garden on one side and extended views to the islands and the sea on the other, has some fine rhododendrons and azaleas with a variety of trees, shrubs, vegetables and flower borders betwen box hedges. Woodland walk. Plant stall, vegetables when available. Oban 13 miles, Easdale 3 miles. 1½ miles of narrow road off B844 to Easdale.

Admission £1.00 Children 50p

Daily 15th MARCH to 31st OCTOBER Other visits by arrangement Tel. 08523 353

Donation to Scotland's Gardens Scheme

ARDUAINE, Kilmelford
(The National Trust for Scotland)

Remarkable coastal garden on a hillside overlooking Loch Melfort and the Sound of Jura. Its internationally famous collection of rhododendron species is mainly sheltered within a Japanese larch woodland while, below, the water garden provides an informal setting for a wide range of trees, shrubs and perennials which thrive in the mild climate of the western seaboard. Located between Oban and Lochgilphead on the A816, sharing an entrance with the Loch Melfort Hotel.

Admission £2.00 Children & OAPs £1.00

SATURDAY & SUNDAY 7th & 8th MAY 9.30 am – 6 pm

40% to NTS Threave Bursary Fund

For details of other openings see page 130

BARGUILLEAN'S "ANGUS GARDEN", Taynuilt
(Mr Sam Macdonald)

Nine acre woodland garden around eleven acre loch set in the Glen Lonan hills. Spring flowering bulbs, extensive collection of rhododendron hybrids, deciduous azaleas, shrubs, primulas and conifers. Garden recently extended by two acres. Access and car park provided. The garden contains the largest collection of North American rhododendron hybrids in the west of Scotland. Coach tours by arrangement: Tel: 08662 333 or Fax: 08662 375. Taynuilt 3 miles.

Admission £1.00 Children free

DAILY ALL YEAR

Donation to Scotland's Gardens Scheme

COILLE DHARAICH, Kilmelford, Oban   &

(Drs Alan & Hilary Hill)

Small garden, centred on natural rock outcrop, pool and scree terraces and troughs. Wide variety of primulas, alpines, dwarf conifers, bulbs, bog and peat loving plants. No dogs please. Plant stall. Half a mile from Kilmelford on road signposted "Degnish".

Admission £1.00 Children free

SATURDAY & SUNDAY 4th & 5th JUNE 2 – 6 pm Other days by arrangement. Tel: (08522) 285

40% to North Argyll Eventide Home Association

COLINTRAIVE GARDENS

Four delightful spring and woodland gardens of varied interest, within easy reach of each other. Set in a scenic corner of Argyll.

1 – **Kinlochruel House** Mr & Mrs T M Mowat

2 – **Dunyvaig** Mrs M Donald

3 – **Tigh-na-bheag** Mr & Mrs J W Morris

4 – **Stronailne** Mr & Mrs H Andrew

Please call at No. 1 for admission tickets and directions. Dogs on lead please. Plant stall. On A886, 20 miles from Dunoon.

Admission £1.50 Children 50p includes all 4 gardens

SATURDAY & SUNDAY 14th and 15th MAY 2 – 6 pm

All takings to Scotland's Gardens Scheme

CRARAE GLEN, Minard, by Inveraray   & (only Lower Gardens)

(Crarae Gardens Charitable Trust)

Rhododendrons, exotic trees and shrubs in a Highland glen. Spectacular spring and autumn colour. Dogs on short lead please. Plant sales. Visitor Centre open 10 am – 5 pm April to October. Open winter during daylight hours. Minard 1 mile. Eleven miles south of Inveraray on A83.

Admission: Fixed charge. Car parking and children under five, free.

Daily APRIL to OCTOBER 9 am – 6 pm. Winter during daylight hours

Donation to Scotland's Gardens Scheme

CRINAN HOTEL GARDEN, Crinan
(Mr & Mrs N Ryan)
Rock garden with azaleas and rhododendrons created into the hillside over a century ago and sheltered, secluded garden with sloping lawns, unexpected herbaceous beds and spectacular views of the canal and Crinan Loch. Teas. Lochgilphead A 83, A816 Oban then A841 Cairnbaan to Crinan.
Admission £1.00 Accompanied children free
TUESDAY & WEDNESDAY 24th & 25th MAY 10am – 6 pm
40% to Mid-Argyll Hospital Fund

DALNAHEISH, Tayvallich
(Mrs C J Lambie)
Small, informal old garden overlooking the Sound of Jura. Woodland, planted rock, shrubs, bulbs, rhododendrons, azaleas and a wide variety of plants from around the world.
Admission by telephone appointment only Tel: 05467 286. Donations. One mile from Tayvallich.
APRIL to OCTOBER by appointment, due to limited car parking
All takings to Scotland's Gardens Scheme

DRUIMAVUIC HOUSE, Appin
(Mr & Mrs Newman Burberry)
Stream, wall and woodland gardens with lovely views over Loch Creran. Spring bulbs, rhododendrons, azaleas, primulas, meconopsis, violas. Dogs on lead please. Plant stall. Route A828 Oban/Fort William, 4 miles south of Appin. Use private road where public signs warn of flooding.
Admission £1.00 Children free
Daily from 17th APRIL to 2nd JULY 10 am – 6 pm
Donation to Scotland's Gardens Scheme

DRUIMNEIL HOUSE, Port Appin
(Mrs J Glaisher)
Ten acre garden overlooking Loch Linnhe with many fine varieties of mature trees and rhododendrons and other woodland shrubs. Home made teas available. Collection box. 2 miles from A828. Connel/Fort William road. Sharp left at Airds Hotel, second house on right.
Admission 50p Children free
Daily from 28th MARCH to 19th JUNE 9 am – 6 pm
All takings to Scotland's Gardens Scheme

GLENFEOCHAN HOUSE HOTEL, Kilmore, by Oban
(Mr & Mrs D Baber)
Over 100 different rhododendrons. Azaleas, specimen trees and tender flowering shrubs. Carpets of spring bulbs and beautiful autumn colours. Walled garden with herbaceous border, herbs, fruit and vegetables. Plant stall. Teas. Produce when available. 5 miles south of Oban at head of Loch Feochan on A816.
Admission £1.50 Children 50p
Daily from 15th MARCH to 31st OCTOBER 10 am – 6 pm
Donation to Scotland's Gardens Scheme

JURA HOUSE, Ardfin, Isle of Jura
(Mr F A Riley-Smith)
Organic walled garden with wide variety of unusual plants and shrubs, including large Australasian collection. Also interesting woodland and cliff walk, spectacular views. Points of historical interest, abundant wild life and flowers. Plant stall. 5 miles from ferry terminal. Ferries to Islay from Kennacraig by Tarbert.
Admission £2.50
OPEN ALL YEAR 9 am – 5 pm
Donation to Scotland's Gardens Scheme

KINLOCHLAICH HOUSE GARDENS, Appin ♿ (Gravel paths sloping)
(Mr D E Hutchison)
Closed Sundays mid-October – March. Walled garden, incorporating the West Highlands' largest Nursery Garden Centre. Display beds of alpines, heathers, primulas, rhododendrons, azaleas and herbaceous plants. Fruiting and flowering shrubs and trees. Route A828. Oban 23 miles, Fort William 27 miles. Bus stops at gate by Police Station. Admission 70p
OPEN DAILY ALL YEAR 9.30 am – 5.30 pm or dusk (except Sundays mid-October to March)
40% to Appin Village Hall Fund

KYLES OF BUTE SMALL GARDENS, Tighnabruaich
Four small gardens in and around Tignabruaich within easy reach of each other. Each garden entirely different with something of interest for everyone. Plant sale.

1 – **Alt Mhor, Auchenlochan**   Mr & Mrs Peter Scott

2 – **The Cottage**   Col & Mrs Peter Halliday

3 – **La Madrugada, Auchenlochan**   Rev & Mrs Patrick Hamilton

4 – **Heatherfield, Kames**   Mr & Mrs David Johnston

Please call at No.1 first for admission tickets and directions. Dogs on lead please.
Admission £1.50 Children 50p includes all 4 gardens
SATURDAY & SUNDAY 21st & 22nd MAY 2 – 6 pm
All takings to Scotland's Gardens Scheme

TAYNUILT GARDENS
CLACH-NA-NESSAIG   (Mrs S B H Thomson)
Established garden with mixed borders and vegetable garden
BIRCHWOOD   (Mrs M R Stoupe)
Development of an old garden with small pond and new rockery.
Both gardens are about three-quarters of an acre, overlooking Loch Etive. Plant stall. Teas. Dogs on lead please. Route: A85 from Oban, $\frac{1}{2}$ mile on Connel side of Taynuilt, sign to Airds Bay. Turn down to Loch Etive. Gardens are the last two houses on this road. Admission £1.00 includes both gardens. Accompanied children free
SATURDAY & SUNDAY 25th & 26th JUNE 2 – 6 pm
40% to Alzheimer's Scotland, Oban & Lorne branch

TIGHNAMARA, Melfort, Kilmelford
(Lt Cmdr & Mrs H D Campbell-Gibson)

Two acre garden set in an ancient oak wood with outstanding views over Loch Melfort. Interesting variety of shrubs and many perennial plants. Paths with terraced beds up hillside. Woodland garden with pool, surrounded by massed primulas, hostas, cranesbill geraniums and astilbes and an abundance of bulbs and wild flowers. Teas. Plant stall. One mile from Kilmelford on lochside road to Degnish.

Amission £1.00 Accompanied children free

SATURDAY & SUNDAY 4th & 5th JUNE 2 – 6 pm. Other visits by appointment any day between Spring and Autumn. Tel: 08522 224.

40% to World Society for the Protection of Animals

TOROSAY CASTLE & GARDENS, Isle of Mull
(Mr Christopher James)

Scottish baronial house (1858) by David Bryce. Twelve acre gardens with statue walk attributed to Sir Robert Lorimer c.1899. Craignure 1½ miles. Route: Steamer six times daily from Oban to Craignure. Miniature steam railway from Craignure ferry. Lochaline to Fishnish, then seven miles south on A849. (See full page advertisement).

Admission £1.50 Children & OAPs £1.00

GARDENS OPEN DAILY ALL YEAR. Summer, 9 am – 7 pm. Winter, sunrise – sunset.
CASTLE OPEN LATE APRIL to MID-OCTOBER (extra admission) 10.30 am – 5 pm

Donation to Scotland's Gardens Scheme

AYRSHIRE
(STRATHCLYDE REGION)

Joint District Organisers:	**Mrs R G Angus,** Ladykirk House, Monkton KA9 2SF
	Mrs J R Findlay, Carnell, Hurlford KA1 5JS
Area Organisers:	**Mrs R F Cuninghame,** Caprington Castle, Kilmarnock KN2 9AA
	Mrs R Y Henderson, Blairston, Ayr KA7 4EF
Hon. Treasurer:	**Mr James McFadzean,** Bank of Scotland, 123 High Street, Ayr KA7 1QP

DATES OF OPENING

Blair, Dalry	All year round	
Culzean Castle & Country Park	Daily April-Oct 10.30am – 5.30pm	
Carnell, Hurlford	Sunday 3 April	2 – 4.30pm
Culzean Castle & Country Park	Sunday 10 April	10.30am – 5.30pm
Culzean Castle & Country Park	Thursday 5 May	10.30am – 5.30pm
Ashcraig, Skelmorlie	Sunday 15 May	2 – 5.30pm
Auchincruive, Ayr	Sunday 22 May	1 – 6pm
Doonholm, Ayr	Sunday 29 May	2 – 5.30pm
Hughenden, Troon	Sunday 19 June	2 – 6pm
Annanhill Nursery	Sunday 26 June	2 – 5pm
Barnweil, Craigie	Sunday 3 July	2 – 6pm
Swallow Ha', Symington	Sunday 10 July	2 – 6pm
Culzean Castle & Country Park	Wed. 20 July	10.30am – 5.30pm
Carnell, Hurlford	Sunday 24 July	2 – 5pm
Barr Village Gardens	Saturday 6 August	1 – 5pm
Skeldon, Dalrymple	Sunday 7 August	2 – 6pm
Blairquhan, Straiton	Sunday 14 August	1.30 – 4.30pm
Lagg House, Dunure	Sunday 21 August	2 – 5pm

ANNANHILL NURSERY, Kilmarnock ♿ (partly)
(Kilmarnock & Loudon District Council)
A chance to view the District Council's nursery complex as well as the walled garden with its herbaceous borders and annual flower beds. Teas. Plant stall. Near Annanhill 18 hole golf course; Annanhill pitch and putt and trampoline have separate charges. Situated in Irvine Road, off Western Road coming from Glasgow or from bypass.
Admission 50p Children free OAPs 25p
SUNDAY 26th JUNE 2 – 5 pm
40% to Provost's Charity Fund

 # ASHCRAIG, Skelmorlie
(Mr & Mrs Richard Yeomans)
Large garden originally laid out in 1820, presently under renovation, consisting of lawns, woodland and formal gardens, walled garden, also informal cottage garden (Ashcraig Cottage – Mr & Mrs C Fisher). Many interesting trees and shrubs including large collection of rhododendrons, azaleas and hydrangeas. Plant stall. Tea & biscuits. Cars free. Skelmorlie approx. $1\frac{1}{2}$ miles on A78 four miles north of Largs.
Admission £1.50 Children 50p
SUNDAY 15th MAY 2 – 5.30 pm
40% Cancer Research Campaign (Scotland)

AUCHINCRUIVE, Ayr ♿
(Scottish Agricultural College)
Classical house of 1764 – 67 built for the Oswald family. Interior decoration by Robert Adam, former tea house also by Robert Adam, 1778. (Tea house not open). Extensive amenity grounds of the College campus, the setting for buildings and other facilities serving all aspects of the educational, research and consultancy work of the College. Attractive riverside gardens with plant display and commercial glasshouses, herbaceous and shrub borders, arboretum and a range of commercial crops, together forming part of a horticultural teaching and research department. Car parking free. Tea and cakes in Oswald Hall. Wide selection of pot plants, shrubs and Auchincruive honey for sale. Ayr 3m. Route B743. Bus: Ayr to Annbank and Tarbolton buses stop at College gate.
Admission £1.50 Children under 14 free OAPs £1.00
SUNDAY 22nd MAY 1 – 6 pm
40% between Erskine Hospital, the Scottish War Blind and British Red Cross Society

BARNWEIL, Craigie, near Kilmarnock ♿
(Mr & Mrs Ronald Alexander)
A relatively new garden still being developed. Woodland walk. Shrub rose and herbaceous borders of various related colours. Cars free. Home baked teas in house. Craigie 2 miles. Route: Right off B730, 2 miles south of A77.
Admission £1.50 Children under 12 free
SUNDAY 3rd JULY 2 – 6 pm
40% to Tarbolton Parish Church

 # BARR VILLAGE GARDENS ♿ (some)
A large number of attractive village gardens, some old, some new, within this small and beautiful conservation village and two about half a mile away. Maps and tickets available at each open garden. Teas in Barr Community Hall. Plant stall. Large nursery garden on outskirts of village. Barr is on B734, Girvan 8 miles, Ballantrae 17 miles.
Admission £1.00 Children and OAPs 50p
SATURDAY 6th AUGUST 1 – 5 pm
40% to the Scottish Children's Hospice

BLAIR, Dalry
(Mrs M G Borwick)
Policies open all year round for walkers.
Donations welcome
OPEN ALL YEAR ROUND
All takings to Scotland's Gardens Scheme

BLAIRQUHAN, Straiton, Maybole   ₰
(Mr James Hunter-Blair)
Castle in Tudor style designed by William Burn, 1820 – 24. Sixty-foot high saloon with gallery. Lintels and sculptured stones from earlier fortified house incorporated in kitchen courtyard. Original furniture and interesting pictures including gallery with collection of Scottish Colourists. Three mile private drive along the River Girvan. Walled garden with herbaceous border. Regency glasshouse, extensive grounds with specimen trees and views. Admission price includes tour of house. Tea in house. Half mile west of Straiton. Entry from B7045.
Admission £3.00 Children & OAPs £2.00
SUNDAY 14th AUGUST 1.30 – 4.30 pm
40% to Architectural Heritage Society

CARNELL, Hurlford   ₰
(Mr & Mrs J R Findlay)
Alterations in 1843 by William Burn. 16th century peel tower. Teas and baking stall. Cars free. Kilmarnock 6 miles. Mauchline 4 miles on A76. 1½ miles on Ayr side of A719.
Admission £1.50
SUNDAY 3rd APRIL 2 – 4.30 pm Daffodil Day.
40% between Multiple Sclerosis Society (Ayrshire) and Malcolm Sargent House, Prestwick
and
Walled garden, rock and water gardens; 100 yards herbaceous borders, also vegetables grown with compost. Electrically heated greenhouses. Flower and plant stalls.
Herbaceous borders around Carnell House with garden craft and home baking stalls. Ice cream and cream teas. Cars free.
Admission £2.00 Children under 12 free
SUNDAY 24th JULY 2 – 5 pm
40% between Army Benevolent Fund and Scottish Conservation Projects Trust

CULZEAN CASTLE, Maybole
(The National Trust for Scotland)
Former tower house, castellated and remodelled by Robert Adam 1779 – 90, complete with viaduct, stables and home farm. Three main garden areas, the Fountain Court (a terraced garden in front of the Castle with an Orangery), the Walled Garden and Herb Garden (herbaceous, semi-tropical trees, shrubs and plants) and Happy Valley (a wild woodland garden with specimen trees and shrubs). Visitor Centre, 18th century castle, deer park, woodland walks, ranger-led excursions, events programme, swan pond and other exhibitions. Combined ticket for Castle & Country Park: Adults £5.50 Concessions £3.00. Country Park: Adults £3.00 Concessions £1.50. Castle only: Adults £3.50 Concessions £1.80. Party rates on application. Restaurant at Visitor Centre. Open daily April – October 10.30 am – 5.30 pm. Maybole 4 miles. Route: A719.
SUNDAY 10th APRIL, THURSDAY 5th MAY & WEDNESDAY 20th JULY
Scotland's Gardens Scheme Tour 2 – 3.30 pm
40% to NTS Threave Bursary Fund
For other opening details see page 133

DOONHOLM, Ayr   ♿ (limited)
(Mr Peter Kennedy)
Informal gardens in attractive setting on the banks of the River Doon. Mature trees, shrubs and marvellous show of rhododendrons and azaleas. Tea and biscuits. Plant stall. Signposted from Burns' Cottage, Alloway and from A77.
Admission £1.50 Children & OAPs 50p
SUNDAY 29th MAY 2 – 5.30 pm
40% between Multiple Sclerosis Society and The Samaritans

HUGHENDEN, Monktonhill Road, Troon   ♿
(Mr & Mrs D Williams)
Seaside garden of four acres. Mainly flowering trees and shrubs. Shrub roses, azaleas and tree lupins. Tea in conservatory. Monktonhill Road runs between Prestwick bypass and Troon. Ayr/Troon buses run along Southwood Road, from where there is walking access to garden via wicket gate.
Admission £1.00 Children free
SUNDAY 19th JUNE 2 – 6 pm
40% to British Red Cross Society (Troon branch)

 # LAGG HOUSE, Dunure   ♿ (mainly)
(Mr & Mrs J Greenall)
Small coastal country garden in process of ongoing renovation. Teas. Plant stall. Take A719 coast road from Ayr, three miles from Doonfoot roundabout.
Admission £1.00 Children under 12 free
SUNDAY 21st AUGUST 2 – 5 pm
40% to Action Research (Maybole branch)

SKELDON, Dalrymple
(Mr S E Brodie QC, & Mrs Brodie)
One and a half acres of formal garden and four acres of woodland garden in unique setting on the banks of the River Doon. Large collection of rhododendrons and azaleas, substantial glasshouse collection. Home baked teas. Silver band on the lawn. Plants for sale. Cars free. Dalrymple, B7034 between Dalrymple and Hollybush.
Admission £1.50 Children & OAPs 50p
SUNDAY 7th AUGUST 2 – 6 pm
40% to the Mental Health Foundation

SWALLOW HA', Symington
(Mr & Mrs Iain Tulloch)
This half acre garden has something of interest around every corner. Bulbs, plants, shrubs and trees ensure year-round colour and variety. Home baked teas available at Hayes Garden Centre. Take B730 west of A77, first left to Symington. Garden 400 yards. No dogs please.
Admission £1.00 Children under 14 free
SUNDAY 10th JULY 2 – 6 pm
40% to The Scottish Dyslexia Trust

BERWICKSHIRE
(BORDERS REGION)

District Organiser:	**The Hon Mrs Charles Ramsay,** Bughtrig, Leitholm, Coldstream TD14 4JP
Area Organisers:	**Lt Col S J Furness,** The Garden House, Netherbyres, Eyemouth TD14 5SE
	Miss Jean Thomson, Stable Cottage, Lambden, Greenlaw, Duns TD10 6UN
Hon. Treasurer:	**Mr James Mackie,** Bank of Scotland, 88 High Street, Coldstream TD12 4AQ

DATES OF OPENING

Bughtrig, Leitholm	May – September	11am – 5pm
The Hirsel, Coldstream	Open daily all year, reasonable daylight hours	
Manderston, Duns	Sundays & Thursdays 5 May – 29 September	

Netherbyres, Eyemouth	Sunday 17 April	2 – 6pm
Sunnyside, Langton Gate, Duns	Sunday 1 May	2 – 5.30pm
Charterhall, Duns	Sunday 22 May	2 – 5pm
Mordington House, Paxton	Sunday 29 May	2 – 6pm
Springhill, Birgham	Sunday 29 May	2 – 6pm
Manderston, Duns	Monday 30 May	2 – 5.30pm
Bughtrig, Leitholm	Sunday 10 July	2.30 – 5.30pm
Netherbyres, Eyemouth	Sunday 17 July	2 – 6pm
Manderston, Duns	Monday 29 August	2 – 5.30pm

BUGHTRIG, Near Leitholm, Coldstream ♿
(Major General & The Hon Mrs Charles Ramsay)
Interesting Georgian house about 1790. New porch, roof balustrades and other features
after 1875. Old roses, shrubs, herbaceous. Cars free. Tea in house. Produce stalls. Small
picnic area available. Quarter mile east of Leitholm on B6461.
Admission £1.00 Children 50p
OPEN DAILY MAY to SEPTEMBER 11am – 5 pm, or by appointment, tel: 0890 840678
SUNDAY 10th JULY 2.30 – 5.30 pm
40% to Leitholm WRI

CHARTERHALL, Duns ♿
(Mr & Mrs Alexander Trotter)
Hybrid rhododendrons and azaleas in mature grounds. Flower garden, surrounding
modern house. Small greenhouse and vegetable garden. Tea with home bakes and
biscuits. Plant stall. 6 miles south west of Duns and 3 miles east of Greenlaw on B6460.
Admission £1.00 Children 50p
SUNDAY 22nd MAY 2 – 5 pm
40% to Christ Church, Duns, Fabric Fund

MANDERSTON, Duns ♿
(The Lord Palmer)
The swan song of the great classical house. Formal and woodland gardens. Tearoom in
grounds. 2 miles east of Duns on A6105. Buses from Galashiels and Berwick. Alight at
entrance on A6105.
SUNDAYS & THURSDAYS 5th MAY to 29th SEPTEMBER,
HOLIDAY MONDAYS 30th MAY and 29th AUGUST 2 – 5.30 pm
Parties any time by appointment.
Donation to Scotland's Gardens Scheme

 # MORDINGTON HOUSE, Paxton
(Mr & Mrs J H Trotter)
Modern house in mature woodland grounds. Hybrid rhododendrons and azaleas.
Recently replanted Garden House and walled garden under reconstruction. Teas and
home bakes. Plant stall. Route: A6105 two miles west of Berwick-on-Tweed, one mile east
of Foulden. Follow signs to Mordington.
Admission £1.00 Children 50p
SUNDAY 29th MAY 2 – 6 pm
20% to Foulden Church and 20% to St Columba's Hospice

NETHERBYRES, Eyemouth ♿
(Lt Col S J Furness & G.R.B.S.)
Unique 18th century elliptical walled garden, with a new house built inside. Daffodils
and wild flowers in the spring. Annuals, roses, herbaceous borders and coloured borders
during the summer. Produce stall. Teas in house. Eyemouth quarter mile on A1107.
Admission £1.50 Children 50p
SUNDAY 17th APRIL 2 – 6 pm
40% to Eyemouth Museum Trust
SUNDAY 17th JULY 2 – 6 pm
40% to St Ebba's Church Funds

SPRINGHILL, Birgham   ♿ (partly)
(Mrs Hogarth)
Historic garden which is being restored. Shrubs, azaleas, views of River Tweed. Teas in house. Exhibition of plans of garden history and restoration. Half mile west of Birgham on A698 Kelso to Coldstream road.
Admission £1.00 Children 50p
SUNDAY 29th MAY 2 – 6 pm
40% to National Art Collection Fund

SUNNYSIDE, Langton Gate, Duns   ♿ (partly)
(Mr & Mrs J Gibson)
Three-quarter acre small country garden, small apple orchard, some interesting shrubs, lawns, vegetables, bulbs, climbers. 1847 Gunstock walnut and old Angelica tree. Himalayan laburnum. Plant stall. Tea and biscuits in house. Well signposted, Duns – West End; Greenlaw Road (A6105); half mile west of town square, below road. Parking available in Duns Castle south gate drive.
Admission £1.00 Children over 12 50p OAPs 50p
SUNDAY 1st MAY 2 – 5.30 pm
40% to Scottish Society for the Prevention of Cruelty to Animals

---

THE HIRSEL, Coldstream   ♿ (partly)
(Lord Home of the Hirsel KT)
Snowdrops and aconites in Spring; daffodils in April/early May; rhododendrons and azaleas in late May/early June, and magnificent autumn colouring. Walks round the lake, Dundock Wood and Leet valley. Marvellous old trees. Dogs on leads, please. Homestead Museum, Craft Centre and Workshops. Tearoom in main season (by appointment for parties). Immediately west of Coldstream on A697. Parking charge only
OPEN DAILY ALL YEAR (Reasonable daylight hours)
Donation to Scotland's Gardens Scheme

CAITHNESS & SUTHERLAND
(HIGHLAND REGION)

Joint District Organisers:	**Mrs Robert Howden,** The Firs, Langwell, Berriedale, Caithness KW7 6HD
	Mrs Victor Grenfell, Stemster, By Halkirk, Caithness KW12 6UX
Area Organiser:	**Mrs Richard Tyser,** Gordonbush, Brora, Sutherland KW9 6LX
Hon. Treasurer:	**Mr H Forbes,** Clydesdale Bank plc, 17 Trail Street, Thurso KW14 7EL

DATES OF OPENING

Dunrobin Castle, Golspie	Saturday 25 June	10.30am – 5.30pm
Castle of Mey	Wednesday 20 July	2 – 6pm
Castle of Mey	Thursday 28 July	2 – 6pm
House of Tongue, Tongue	Saturday 30 July	2 – 6pm
Sandside House Gardens, by Reay	Saturday 6 August	2.30pm
Langwell, Berriedale	Sunday 7 August	2 – 6pm
Langwell, Berriedale	Sunday 14 August	2 – 6pm
Dunbeath Castle, Caithness	Sunday 21 August	2 – 6pm
Castle of Mey	Friday 2 September	2 – 6pm

CASTLE OF MEY, Mey, Caithness &

(H.M. Queen Elizabeth The Queen Mother)

Z-plan castle formerly the seat of the Earls of Caithness. 18th and 19th century additions. Remodelled 1954. Old walled-in garden. On north coast and facing the Pentland Firth and Orkney. Cars free. Teas served under cover. Mey $1\frac{1}{2}$ miles. Route A836. Bus: Please enquire at local bus depots. Special buses can be arranged.

Admission £1.50 Children under 12 £1.00 OAPs £1.00

WEDNESDAY 20th JULY 2 – 6 pm

40% to Scottish Disability Foundation (Edinburgh)

THURSDAY 28th JULY and FRIDAY 2nd SEPTEMBER 2 – 6 pm

40% to Queen's Nursing Institute (Scotland)

DUNBEATH CASTLE, Dunbeath &

(Mr & Mrs R Stanton Avery)

Traditional walled garden recently re-landscaped and containing magnificent display of herbaceous and greenhouse plants, together with vegetable garden and heather corner. Short woodland walk. Teas served in former coach house. Route: A9 to Dunbeath village Post Office, then follow old A9 south for $1\frac{1}{4}$ miles to castle gates.

Admission £1.50 Children under 12 50p OAPs 50p

SUNDAY 21st AUGUST 2 – 6 pm

40% to Arthritis and Rheumatism Council for Research (Scotland)

DUNROBIN CASTLE & GARDENS, Golspie

(The Sutherland Trust)

Formal gardens laid out in 1850 by the architect, Barry. Set beneath the fairytale castle of Dunrobin. Tearoom and gift shop in castle. Picnic site and woodland walks. Dunrobin Castle Museum in the gardens. Suitable for disabled by prior arrangement. Group admission: Adults £3.00, children £1.50, family £8.00. Castle one mile north of Golspie on A9.

Admission £3.20 Children £1.60 OAPs £2.10

SATURDAY 25th JUNE 10.30 am – 5.30 pm. (Last admission 5 pm)

40% to The British Lung Foundation

HOUSE OF TONGUE, Tongue, Lairg & (partially)

(The Countess of Sutherland)

17th century house on Kyle of Tongue. Walled garden, herbaceous borders, old fasioned roses. Teas available at the Ben Loyal and Tongue Hotels. Tongue half a mile. House just off main road approaching causeway.

Admission to garden £1.00 Children 50p

SATURDAY 30th JULY 2 – 6 pm

40% to Royal Society for the Prevention of Cruelty to Children

---

LANGWELL, Berriedale &

(The Lady Anne Bentinck)

A beautiful old walled-in garden situated in the secluded Langwell strath. Charming access drive with a chance to see deer. Cars free. Teas served under cover. Berriedale 2 miles. Route A9. Please enquire at bus depots in Wick and Thurso for buses.

Admission £1.50 Children under 12 £1.00 OAPs £1.00

SUNDAY 7th AUGUST 2 – 6 pm

40% to RNLI

SUNDAY 14th AUGUST 2 – 6 pm

40% to RNLI

SANDSIDE HOUSE GARDENS by Reay, Thurso ♿ (partially)

(Mr & Mrs Geoffrey Minter)

Old walled gardens being restored but well stocked. Sunken rectangular walled garden. Upper garden with sea views to the Orkneys and Grade A listed 2-seater privy. Terrace with rockery overlooking sunken garden. Main gate is on A836 half mile west of Reay village. Teas. Plant stall. There is a splayed entrance with railings and gate lodge. Admission £1.25 Children under 5 free

SATURDAY 6th AUGUST 2.30pm

40% to Reay Church Hall

CENTRAL
(CENTRAL REGION)

District Organiser:	**Lady Edmonstone,** Duntreath Castle, Blanefield G83 9AJ
Area Organisers:	**Mrs John Carr,** Duchray Castle, Aberfoyle FK8 3XL
	Mrs Guy Crawford, St Blanes House, Dunblane FK15 0ER
	Mrs Robin Hunt, Keirhill, Balfron G83 0LG
	Mrs John Stein, Southwood, Southfield Crescent, Stirling FK8 2QJ
	Mrs Patrick Stirling-Aird, Old Kippenross, Dunblane FK15 0CQ
	The Hon Mrs R E G Younger, Old Leckie, Gargunnock FK8 3BN
Hon. Treasurer:	**Mrs I M Taylor,** Royal Bank of Scotland, 82 Murray Place, Stirling FK8 2DR

DATES OF OPENING

Blairhoyle, Port of Menteith	Wednesdays April-September 1 – 5pm	
Kilbryde Castle, Dunblane	By appointment	
Kilbryde Castle, Dunblane	Sunday 13 March	2 – 4pm
Kilbryde Castle, Dunblane	Sunday 10 April	2 – 5pm
Norrieston House, Thornhill	Wednesday 27 April	2 – 5.30pm
Kilbryde Castle, Dunblane	Sunday 1 May	2 – 5pm
Touch, Cambusbarron	Sunday 15 May	2 – 5pm
Norrieston House, Thornhill	Wednesday 18 May	2 – 5.30pm
Duchray Castle, Aberfoyle	Sun & Mon 29/30 May	2 – 5pm
Duntreath Castle, Blanefield	Sunday 5 June	2 – 5.30pm
Kilbryde Castle, Dunblane	Sunday 5 June	2 – 5pm
Pass House, Kilmahog	Sunday 5 June	2 – 5.30pm
Norrieston House, Thornhill	Sunday 12 June	2 – 5.30pm
The Blair, Blairlogie	Sunday 12 June	2 – 5pm
Norrieston House, Thornhill	Wednesday 22 June	2 – 5.30pm
Kilbryde Castle, Dunblane	Sunday 10 July	2 – 5pm
Menteith House, Port of Menteith	Sunday 10 July	2 – 5.30pm
Norrieston House, Thornhill	Wednesday 13 July	2 – 5.30pm
Cambusmore, Callander	Sunday 24 July	2 – 5.30pm
Orchardlea House, Callander	Sat & Sun 13/14 August	2 – 5.30pm
Kilbryde Castle, Dunblane	Sunday 14 August	2 – 5pm
Kilbryde Castle, Dunblane	Sunday 11 September	2 – 5pm
Kilbryde Castle, Dunblane	Sunday 9 October	2 – 5pm

BLAIRHOYLE, Port of Menteith
(Col & Mrs J D Pattullo)

Exceptional garden leading down through mature arboretum to landscaped lake. Wide variety of shrubs and plants, azaleas, heathers, dwarf conifers, roses, primulas and well planted rockery. Dogs on lead, please. Route: A837 between Thornhill and Port of Menteith.

Admission £1.00

EVERY WEDNESDAY APRIL to SEPTEMBER inclusive 1 – 5 pm

40% to Strathcarron Hospice

CAMBUSMORE, Callander &
(Captain & Mrs J N B Baillie-Hamilton)

Two acre walled garden. Shrub border. Extensive lawns, parkland, policy wood and river walk. Plant stall. Cake stall. Teas. Cambusmore – 2 miles east of Callander on A84.

Admission £1.50 Children 50p

SUNDAY 24th JULY 2 – 5.30 pm

40% to Strathcarron Hospice

DUCHRAY CASTLE, Aberfoyle &
(Mr & Mrs John Carr)

16th century castle, isolated in dramatic countryside, overlooking Duchray water. Small, formal garden; renovated rock garden; lawns and rhododendrons. Woodland walk through massed bluebells. Cream teas. Plant stall. Route: 2 miles west of Aberfoyle through Queen Elizabeth Forest Park. Free minibus transport available from outside Aberfoyle Tourist Office.

Admission £1.50 Children & OAPs 50p

SUNDAY & MONDAY 29th & 30th MAY 2 – 5 pm

40% to Crossroads Care

DUNTREATH CASTLE, Blanefield &
(Sir Archibald Edmonstone)

Extensive gardens with mature and new plantings. Newly landscaped lake, water and bog gardens. Formal garden, rhododendrons and woodland walk. 15th century keep and chapel. Pipe band. Dog agility display. Plant, home cooking and bric-a-brac stalls. Home made teas. Route: A81 north of Glasgow between Blanefield and Killearn.

Admission £1.50 Children free

SUNDAY 5th JUNE 2 – 5.30 pm

40% between Strathclyde Youth Clubs and Riding for the Disabled

KILBRYDE CASTLE, Dunblane, Perthshire & (partly)
(Sir Colin & Lady Campbell & Mr J Fletcher)

Traditional Scottish baronial house rebuilt 1877 to replace building dating from 1461. Partly mature gardens with additions and renovations since 1970. Lawns overlooking Ardoch Burn with wood and water garden still to be completed. Three miles from Dunblane and Doune, signposted from both. No teas. No dogs. Children to be controlled. No toilets. Plants usually for sale.

Admission £1.50

SUNDAYS 13th MARCH 2 – 4 pm, 10th APRIL, 1st MAY, 5th JUNE, 10th JULY, 14th AUGUST, 11th SEPTEMBER, 9th OCTOBER 2 – 5pm.
Also by appointment. Tel: 0786 823104

40% to Leighton Library, Strathcarron Hospice, Cancer Relief Macmillan Fund and the Friends of Dunblane Cathedral.

MENTEITH HOUSE, Port of Menteith ♿

(Mrs R A Gwyn)

Delightful garden sloping down to the Lake of Menteith with fine views to Inchmaholme Priory and island. Well cultivated herbaceous and vegetable gardens. Good variety of roses. Home produce stall. Varied and expert plant stall. Home made teas. Port of Menteith is between Aberfoyle and Thornhill on A81. House is next door to the Lake Hotel.

Admission £1.50 Small children free OAPs £1.00

SUNDAY 10th JULY 2 – 5.30 pm

40% to Donkey Driving for the Disabled

NORRIESTON HOUSE, Thornhill

(Mr & Mrs Robin Price)

South facing village garden, looking to the Gargunnock Hills, created from a field during last six years. Good collection of spring and summer herbaceous plants. Roses and shrubs. Plant stall. From Stirling take A84 to Blair Drummond. Follow A873 to Thornhill, garden situated opposite church. Not suitable for the disabled. Teas on 12th June only.

Admission £1.00 Children free

WEDNESDAYS 27th APRIL & 22nd JUNE 2 – 5.30 pm

40% to Thornhill New Village Hall

WEDNESDAYS 18th MAY & 13 JULY 2 – 5.30 pm

40% to Riding for the Disabled (Sauchieburn Appeal)

SUNDAY 12th JUNE 2 – 5.30 pm.

40% to Norrieston Church

ORCHARDLEA HOUSE, Callander ♿

(Mr & Mrs R B Gunkel)

A "secret" garden of one-third acre framed by fine mature trees and containing an interesting variety of plants and shrubs. Double terrace with herb garden. Plant stall. Teas. Sorry, no dogs. Route: at east end of Callander, 5 minutes walk from centre of village. Disabled parking only.

Admission £1.00 Accompanied children free

SATURDAY & SUNDAY 13th & 14th AUGUST 2 – 5.30 pm

40% to Chest, Heart & Stroke Association (Scotland)

PASS HOUSE, Kilmahog, Callander ♿ (Partly)

(Dr & Mrs D Carfrae)

Rhododendrons, azaleas, wisteria, magnolia, alpines, garden pool, riverside walk, bridge to island. Newly planted flower garden and new propagating house. Swift river with steep banks goes through garden. Plant stall. Teas. Route: 2 miles from Callander on main road A85 to Lochearnhead, one mile from Woollen Mill.

Admission £1.00 Children & OAPs 50p

SUNDAY 5th JUNE 2 – 5.30 pm

40% to Crossroads Care

THE BLAIR, Blairlogie   ♿ (some difficult hills)
(Mr & Mrs Gavin Dobson)
Small 16th century castle set in terraced gardens overlooking the carse. Mature
magnolias, camellias, rhododendrons and azaleas. Cascade fed from stream tumbling
from the Ochils. Delightful mix of mature and interesting new planting. Teas. Half a mile
east of the Wallace monument on A91 near Stirling. Park at roadside car park, just east of
village road and walk up to house.
Admission £1.00 Children & OAPs 50p
SUNDAY 12th JUNE 2 – 5 pm
40% to the Royal Society for the Prevention of Cruelty to Children

---

TOUCH, Cambusbarron   ♿ (partly)
(Mr & Mrs Patrick Buchanan)
Exceptionally fine Georgian house (also open – Admission £1.00) with superb interior.
Interesting old documents and plans. Walled garden with mixed herbaceous and shrub
borders, dwarf rhododendrons, magnolias and many other interesting shrubs. Garden
continually expanding. Easy woodland walk with specie rhododendrons. Plant stall.
Simple teas available.
Admission £2.00 Children & OAPs £1.00
SUNDAY 15th MAY 2 – 5 pm
40% to the National Trust for Scotland

CLYDESDALE
(STRATHCLYDE REGION)

District Organiser:	**Mrs J S Mackenzie,** The Old Manse, Elsrickle, Lanarkshire ML12 6QZ
Area Organisers:	**Miss A V Mackenzie,** Kippit Farm, Dolphinton, West Linton EH46 7HH
	Mrs M Maxwell Stuart, Baitlaws, Lamington, Lanarkshire ML12 6HR
	Mrs John Thomson, Hexagon House, Bardowie Loch, Glasgow G62 6EY
Hon. Treasurer:	**Mr M J Prime,** Elmsleigh, Broughton Road, Biggar, Lanarkshire ML12 6AM

DATES OF OPENING

Biggar Park, Biggar .... By appointment

Nemphlar Garden Trail, Lanark .... Sunday 5 June	2 – 5.30pm
Lawhead Croft, Tarbrax .... Sunday 19 June	2 – 6pm
Kittoch Mill, Carmunnock .... Sunday 26 June	2 – 5pm
Biggar Park, Biggar .... Sunday 10 July	2 – 6pm
Lawhead Croft, Tarbrax .... Sunday 17 July	2 – 6pm
The Old Manse, Elsrickle .... Sunday 24 July	2 – 6pm
Baitlaws, Lamington, and **Glenbreck,** Coulter .... Sunday 31 July	2 – 6pm
Six Fathoms, Eaglesham .... Sunday 7 August	2 – 5pm
Culter Allers, Coulter .... Sunday 7 August	2 – 6pm
17 Dougalston Avenue, Milngavie......................... Saturday 20 August	2 – 5pm

17 DOUGALSTON AVENUE, Milngavie
(Ian G Walls NDH)
A half-acre south sloping suburban garden owned and developed by a former horticultural advisor and author of many books on gardening topics. The garden contains shrubs, lawns, bedding plants and vegetables, fruit and greenhouses. Teas. Plant stall. Dougalston Avenue is off the main A81 Aberfoyle road called 'Glasgow Road'. Turning opposite petrol station.
Admission £1.00 Children over 12 50p OAPs £1.00
SATURDAY 20th AUGUST 2 – 5 pm
40% Cancer Research Campaign

BAITLAWS, Lamington, Biggar
(Mr & Mrs M Maxwell Stuart)
The garden has been developed over the past twelve years with a particular emphasis on colour combinations of hardy shrubs and herbaceous plants, many unusual. Set at around 900 ft above sea level, there are magnificent views of the surrounding hills. Large and varied plant stall. Teas. Route: off A702 above Lamington village. Biggar 5 miles, Abington 5 miles, Lanark 10 miles.
JOINT OPENING WITH GLENBRECK, Coulter.
Admission £1.20 Children over 12 25p
SUNDAY 31st JULY 2 – 6 pm
40% to Biggar Museum Trust

BIGGAR PARK, Biggar & (partially)
(Captain & Mrs David Barnes)
Ten acre garden, starred in the 1994 Good Gardens Guide, incorporating traditional walled garden with large stretches of herbaceous borders, and shrubberies as well as fruit, vegetables and greenhouses. Lawns, walks, pools and many other interesting features, including glades of rhododendrons, azaleas and blue poppies in May and June. Good collection of old fashioned and new specie roses flower in July. Lots of interesting young trees. Home made teas. Plants for sale. 1/4 mile west of Biggar. Buses from Peebles, Dumfries, Edinburgh, etc. stop at front gates. Groups welcome by appointment. Tel: 0899 20185.
Admission £1.50 Children 50p
SUNDAY 10th JULY 2 – 6 pm
40% to Multiple Sclerosis Society

CULTER ALLERS, Coulter & (partially)
(McCosh Brothers)
The one acre Victorian kitchen garden was, until recently, used for the purpose for which it was built, i.e. the growing of garden produce for the house. The garden was re-designed three years ago such that one half of the garden is still for the growing of vegetables and fruit and the other half comprises a lawn and extended, mainly herbaceous, borders. The well, which used to provide water for the original house located in the garden, was uncovered and is now a feature. The remainder of the grounds are open and include a woodland walk. Two or three interesting vehicles on view, weather permitting. Teas. Plant stall. In the village of Coulter 3 miles south of Biggar on A702.
Admission £1.20 Children 25p
SUNDAY 7th AUGUST 2 – 6 pm
40% to Cot Death Society

GLENBRECK, Coulter, Biggar

(Mr & Mrs H M Paterson)
Small, mainly herbaceous, garden beside Culter Water in a conservation village.
Admission by collecting box. Teas in Culter Library. Parking at Culter Mill Restaurant. 3
miles west of Biggar on A702.
JOINT OPENING WITH BAITLAWS, Lamington
SUNDAY 31st JULY 2 – 6 pm
40% to Culter Library

KITTOCH MILL, Carmunnock

(Colonel & Mrs H A Jordan)
Garden contains Scottish National Collection of hostas, about 250 different kinds.
Woodland walk. Waterfall. Many other unusual plants. Teas in Castlemilk Hall in village.
Carmunnock, off Busby to Carmunnock road (B759). Please park on Busby Road.
Admission £1.00 Children 50p
SUNDAY 26th JUNE 2 – 5pm
40% to NCCPG (Strathclyde Group)

LAWHEAD CROFT, Tarbrax　&

(Sue & Hector Riddell)
Cottage, 945 ft above sea level in open Lanarkshire countryside; $1\frac{1}{2}$ acres garden
subdivided into enclosures. Some mature, some new with alpine, bonsai, herbaceous,
fruit, vegetables and pools, full of surprises – we're plant enthusiasts. Plants for sale. No
dogs please. Route: A70, 12 miles from Balerno, 6 miles from Carnwath and Forth.
Signposted from Tarbrax turning.
Admission £1.50 Children 20p
SUNDAY 19th JUNE and SUNDAY 17th JULY 2 – 6 pm. Home baked teas by
Auchengray ladies.
40% to Auchengray & District Charitable Assn. (Church Hall windows)

NEMPHLAR GARDEN TRAIL, Lanark

Several gardens, medium-sized and small, old and new. Late rhododendrons, primulas,
meconopsis, bulbs, flowering shrubs. Teas in Village Hall. Plant stall. Tickets available to
cover all gardens available at car park, or at any of the gardens. $1\frac{1}{2}$ miles north of Lanark
off A73.
Admission £1.50
SUNDAY 5th JUNE 2 – 5.30 pm
40% to The Scottish Children's Hospice

SIX FATHOMS, Eaglesham　& (partly)

(Mr & Mrs A Bewick)
A really useful garden with a little of everything – flowers, fruit, vegetables and a pond.
Plant stall. B767 from Glasgow and East Kilbride.
Admission £1.00 Children over 12 50p OAPs £1.00
SUNDAY 7th AUGUST 2 – 5 pm
40% to Eastpark Home for Children

THE OLD MANSE, Elsrickle, Nr Biggar
(Mrs J S Mackenzie)
Walled garden over 900ft with large herbaceous borders and a wide variety of plants, many unusual, and several rockeries with delphiniums of special interest in July. The garden is situated between the Pentland Hills and the Southern Uplands and enjoys extensive views. Home baked teas. Plants for sale. On A721, 4 miles from Biggar. Admission £1.20 Children over 12 25p
SUNDAY 24th JULY 2 – 6 pm
40% to Blackmount Parish Fabric Appeal Fund

DUMBARTON
(STRATHCLYDE REGION)

District Organiser: **Mrs W A C Reynolds,** North Stanley Lodge, Cove, Helensburgh G84 0NY

Area Organisers: **Mrs W J Angus,** Braeriach, 4 Upper Colquhoun Street, Helensburgh G84 9AH

Mrs F T Crossling, 28 North Grange Road, Bearsden, Glasgow G61 3AF

Mrs James Dykes, Dawn, 42 East Abercromby Street, Helensburgh G84 9JA

Mrs R C Hughes, Brambletye, Argyll Road, Kilcreggan, G84 0JY

Mrs J S Lang, Ardchapel, Shandon, Helensburgh G84 8NP

Hon. Treasurer: **Mr D G D Ryder-Turner,** Letter Cottage, Cove, Helensburgh G84 0NZ

DATES OF OPENING

Glenarn, Rhu	Daily 21 March – 21 June, sunrise to sunset	
Auchendarroch, Tarbet	By appointment	
Old Court, Rhu	Sunday 10 April	2 – 5pm
Glenarn, Rhu	Sunday 1 May	2 – 5.30pm
Askival, Kilcreggan	Sunday 8 May	2 – 5.30pm
Auchendarroch, Tarbet	Sunday 15 May	2 – 5.30pm
Geilston House, Cardross	Saturday 21 May	2 – 5.30pm
Old Court, Rhu	Sunday 22 May	2 – 5pm
Ross Priory, Gartocharn	Sunday 29 May	2 – 6pm
The Linn Garden, Cove	Sunday 5 June	2 – 6pm
Wards, Gartocharn	Sunday 12 June	2 – 6pm
Old Court, Rhu	Sunday 3 July	2 – 5pm
The Hill House, Helensburgh	Sunday 4 September	11am – 5pm

ASKIVAL, Argyll Road, Kilcreggan
(Mr & Mrs D W Geyer)
A largely woodland garden of one and three quarter acres, built on a hillside with views to Arran. Ten years in the making with over 400 interesting trees and shrubs including rhododendrons and many different types of eucalyptus and willows. Lily pond, bog garden and DIY bonsai collection. Cream teas and baking stall at Tighnacraig, next door. Plant stall. Approaching from Garelochhead on B833, turn right along Argyll Road. Askival is 0.8 miles along on left hand side.
Admission £1.00 Children 50p
SUNDAY 8th MAY 2 – 5.30 pm
40% to SSPCA

AUCHENDARROCH, Tarbet
(Mrs Hannah Stirling)
Five acre garden, superbly set on shores of Loch Lomond. Wild garden, woodland walk, wide range of heathers, flowering trees and shrubs including cherries, rhododendrons and azaleas. Regal pelargoniums particularly notable. Plant stall. Baking stall. Raffle. Cup of tea and biscuit in garage. Dogs on lead only. Immediately south of Tarbet on A82, lower entrance gate beside Tarbet Pier.
Admission £1.00 Children free
SUNDAY 15th MAY 2 – 5.30 pm. Other days by appointment. Tel: 03012 240
40% to "The Friends of Loch Lomond"

GEILSTON HOUSE, Cardross   &
(Miss M E Bell)
L-shaped house of one and two storeys. Additions of about 1830. Walled garden. Glen with burn. Azaleas, rhododendrons and flowering shrubs. Wild hyacinths. Provision and plant stall. Sorry no dogs. Cars free. Tea, biscuits and cake in house. Cardross 1 mile. Route A814.
Admission £1.50 Children under 12 free
SATURDAY 21st MAY 2 – 5.30 pm
40% to PDSA

GLENARN, Rhu, Dunbartonshire
(Mr & Mrs Michael Thornley & Family)
Woodland garden with burn, daffodils, primulas and bluebells by season, amongst a notable collection of rhododendrons, species and hybrids, as well as magnolias, embothriums and many other fine trees and shrubs. Restoration work in progress at the old pond. Collecting box. Dogs on lead please. No cars up drive. A814 between Helensburgh and Garelochhead. Regular bus service, stop at Rhu Marina, up Pier Road to Glenarn Road.
Minimum Donation £1.00 Children 50p
OPEN DAILY from First Day of Spring (21st MARCH) to Midsummer's Day (21st JUNE), sunrise – sunset
Donation to Scotland's Gardens Scheme
Special Opening SUNDAY 1st MAY 2 – 5.30 pm. Home made teas and plant stall.
Admission £1.50 Children 50p
40% to Eastend Carers Action Group.

OLD COURT, Artarman Road, Rhu
(Mr & Mrs George Jeffrey)
Small garden with year round interest – herbaceous border, water garden, shrubs, roses, rhododendrons, daffodils. Plant stall. Sorry no dogs. 1½ miles from Helensburgh on A814 towards Rhu. Bus stop opposite Rhu marina.
Admission £1.00 Children free
SUNDAYS 10th APRIL, 22nd MAY, 3rd JULY 2 – 5 pm
Donation to Scotland's Gardens Scheme

ROSS PRIORY, Gartocharn &
(University of Strathclyde)
1812 Gothic addition by James Gillespie Graham to house of 1693 overlooking Loch Lomond. Rhododendrons, azaleas, selected shrubs and trees. Walled garden with glasshouses, alpine beds, pergola, ornamental plantings. Family burial ground. Nature and garden trails. Putting Green. Baking and plant stalls. Tea and biscuits in house. House not open to view. Cars free. Gartocharn 1½ miles off A811. Bus: Balloch to Gartocharn leaves Balloch at 1 pm and 3 pm.
Admission £1.50 Children free
SUNDAY 29th MAY 2 – 6 pm
20% to Scottish Society for the Mentally Handicapped
20% to Scottish Down's Syndrome Association

THE HILL HOUSE, Helensburgh & (garden only)
(The National Trust for Scotland)
SCOTLAND'S GARDENS SCHEME PLANT SALE in garden.
The Hill House overlooking the estuary of the River Clyde, is considered the finest example of the domestic architecture of Charles Rennie Mackintosh. The gardens are being restored to Walter W Blackie's design with features reflecting the work of Mackintosh.
Admission to Plant Sale free. Donations to SGS welcome
SUNDAY 4th SEPTEMBER 11 am – 5 pm

 # THE LINN GARDEN, Cove
(Dr Jim Taggart)
Extensive collections of trees, shrubs, bamboos and water plants surrounding a classical Victorian villa with fine views over the Firth of Clyde. The Linn nursery attached to the garden will be open as usual for the sale of plants and 20% of the afternoon's takings will be donated to Scotland's Gardens Scheme. Teas. Dogs on leads welcome. Entrance 1,100 yards north of Cove village on Shore Road, B833. No parking on avenue, please park on shore side of main road.
Admission £1.00 Children & OAPs 50p
SUNDAY 5th JUNE 2 – 6 pm
40% to Gardeners' Royal Benevolent Society

WARDS, Gartocharn   ♿ (partially)
(Sir Raymond & Lady Johnstone)
Interesting informal garden with mixed borders and water plants alongside natural streams and ponds in a unique setting. Garden merges into Loch Lomond National Nature Reserve. Walks through wild garden and to River Endrick and loch. Bird watching hide. Teas on house terrace or under cover. Plant stall. Sorry no dogs, because of birds. Also open: WARDS COTTAGE (by kind permission of Lady Robert Crichton-Stuart) Interesting cottage garden. Entrance off A811, $2\frac{1}{2}$ miles west of Drymen 1 mile east of Gartocharn village.
Admission £1.50 Children free
SUNDAY 12th JUNE 2 – 6 pm
40% to SSPCA Milton Animal Welfare Centre

DUMFRIES
(DUMFRIES & GALLOWAY REGION)

District Organiser: **Mrs Alison Graham,** Peilton, Moniaive, Thornhill DG3 4HE

Area Organisers: **Miss E Birkbeck,** Glenstuart, Cummertrees,
         Annan DG12 5QA

         Mrs Hew Carruthers, Sidings Cottage, Jardine Hall,
         Lockerbie DG11 1EJ

         Mrs M Johnson-Ferguson, Springkell, Eaglesfield

Hon. Treasurer: **Mrs S Marchbank,** Chintz & China, East Morton Street,
         Thornhill DG3 5IX

DATES OF OPENING

Arbigland, Kirkbean .... Tuesdays to Sundays:
                                 May - September   2 – 6pm
                                 Also Bank Holiday Mondays

Barjarg Tower, Auldgirth .... Sunday 10 April   2 – 5pm
Crichton Royal, Dumfries .... Sunday 15 May   2 – 5pm
Cowhill Tower, Holywood .... Sunday 22 May   2 – 5pm
Dalswinton House, Dalswinton .... Sunday 29 May   2 – 5pm
Sanquhar House, Sanquhar .... Sunday 12 June   2 – 5pm
Kirkland, Courance, Parkgate .... Sunday 19 June   2 – 5pm

ARBIGLAND, Kirkbean
(Captain & Mrs J B Blackett)
Woodland, formal and water gardens arranged round a secluded bay. The garden where Admiral John Paul Jones worked as a boy in the 18th century. Cars free. Picnic area by sandy beach. Dogs on lead, please. Home baked tea in rustic tea room. Signposted on A710 Solway Coast Road.
Admission £2.00 Children over 5 50p OAPs £1.50
TUESDAYS TO SUNDAYS: MAY – SEPTEMBER 2 – 6 pm.
ALSO BANK HOLIDAY MONDAYS
Donation to Scotland's Gardens Scheme

BARJARG TOWER, Auldgirth
(Mr & Mrs J A Donaldson)
16th century tower with later additions. Daffodils. Teas under cover. Car parking free. Route: 4 miles north of Auldgirth on Auldgirth-Penpont Road.
Admission £1.50 Accompanied children 50p
SUNDAY 10th APRIL 2 – 5 pm
40% to St John's Church, Dumfries

COWHILL TOWER, Holywood
(Captain & Mrs A E Weatherall)
Splendid views from lawn down Nith Valley. Interesting walled garden. Topiary animals, birds and figures. Woodland walks. Produce stall. Tea under cover. Holywood 1½ miles, off A76 5 miles north of Dumfries.
Admission £2.00
SUNDAY 22nd MAY 2 – 5 pm
20% to Carnsalloch Cheshire Homes
20% to British Red Cross Society

CRICHTON ROYAL, Dumfries
(The Unit General Manager)
Church and other buildings in beautiful and extensive grounds, containing flowering trees and shrubs, plant centre, rock garden and greenhouses with floral display. Cars free. Tea at Easterbrook Hall. Route: B725, Dumfries 1½ miles.
Admission £1.50 Children 50p
SUNDAY 15th MAY 2 – 5 pm
40% to Crichton Royal Amenity Fund

DALSWINTON HOUSE, Auldgirth
(Sir David & Lady Landale)
Woodland and lochside walks. Cake and plant stall. Home baked teas. Dumfries 7 miles. Bus: Dumfries/Auldgirth via Kirkton. Stop at lodge.
Admission £1.50
SUNDAY 29th MAY 2 – 5 pm
40% to Kirkmahoe Parish Church

KIRKLAND, Courance, Parkgate
(Mr & Mrs R M Graham)
Walled garden. New rock garden. Natural woodland gardens with ponds and young trees on a conservation theme. Teas. Art exhibition. Route: A701 1½ miles north of Parkgate. Halfway between Moffat and Dumfries. Parking in farmyard.
Admission £1.50
SUNDAY 19th JUNE 2 – 5 pm
40% to Marie Curie Cancer Care

SANQUHAR HOUSE, Sanquhar
(Mrs Catriona Murley)
Old manse walled garden. Mature trees and new borders including clematis, old roses and unusual hardy perennials. Teas. Cake and plant stalls. Car parking free. On A76 three-quarters mile north of Sanquhar opposite Sanquhar Academy.
Admission £1.50 Children 50p
SUNDAY 12th JUNE 2 – 5 pm
40% to Arthritis Research

EAST LOTHIAN
(LOTHIAN REGION)

District Organiser:	**Mrs M Burn,** Staneford, Athelstaneford, EH39 5BE
Area Organisers:	**Lady Fraser,** Shepherd House, Inveresk, Musselburgh EH21 7TH
	Lady Malcolm, Whiteholm, Whim Road, Gullane EH31 2BD
	Mrs P Thomson, 1 Westerdunes Court, North Berwick EH39 5DB

DATES OF OPENING

Shepherd House, Inveresk .... Thursday to Sunday 5 – 8 May   2 – 5.30pm
Exhibition of Botanical Paintings

Winton House, Pencaitland .... Sunday 17 April	2 – 6pm
Dirleton Village .... Sat & Sun 23/24 April	2 – 6pm
Colstoun, Haddington .... Sunday 1 May	2 – 5pm
Lennoxlove, Haddington .... Sunday 15 May	10am – 5pm
Stenton Village Gardens .... Sunday 22 May	2 – 6pm
Tyninghame, Dunbar .... Sunday 29 May	2 – 6pm
Houston Mill, East Linton .... Sunday 5 June	10am – 6pm
Shepherd House, Inveresk .... Thursday 9 June	2 – 5.30pm
Bowerhouse, Spott, Dunbar .... Sunday 19 June	2 – 6pm
Luffness, Aberlady .... Sunday 26 June	2 – 6pm
Forbes Lodge, Gifford .... Sunday 3 July	2 – 6pm
Inveresk, near Musselburgh .... Sunday 10 July	2 – 6pm

BOWERHOUSE, Spott, Dunbar   ♿ (weather permitting)
(Ian & Moira Marrian)
Bowerhouse is set in 26 acres of garden, orchard and woodland walks. There is an 18th century walled garden which is filled with a wide variety of flowers and shrubs, fruit and vegetables. Within the grounds, you can also find a doocot, wells, a pets graveyard and farmyard animals. Wildlife is attracted by thoughtful planting. The plant stall is being produced by the NCCPG Lothians group and will have many plants not easily available and a large selection of hardy geraniums. Home made teas. Route: Turn south at the Dunbar A1 bypass sign, Bourhouse/Broomhouse and follow signs for ½ mile.
Admission £1.50 Children 50p OAPs/NCCPG members £1.00 Family ticket £3.50
SUNDAY 19th JUNE 2 – 6 pm
40% to Save the Children Fund

 # COLSTOUN, Haddington
(Madam Broun Lindsay of Colstoun)
Extensive lawns. Rhododendron walk and many fine trees and shrubs. No dogs please. Take turning to Bolton from Haddington/Gifford road. First entrance on left after a bridge.
Admission £1.50 Children & OAPs £1.00
SUNDAY 1st MAY 2 – 5 pm
40% to Guide Dogs for the Blind

DIRLETON VILLAGE   ♿
Small gardens in beautiful village of outstanding architectural interest. Historic kirk. Plant stall. Teas.
Admission £2.50 (includes all gardens) Children 10p
SATURDAY & SUNDAY 23rd & 24th APRIL 2 – 6 pm
40% to Dirleton Kirk

FORBES LODGE, Gifford
(Lady Maryoth Hay)
Water garden. Old fashioned shrub roses. Burn. Stalls. Rare plants. Tea.
Admission £1.00
SUNDAY 3rd JULY 2 – 6 pm
40% to Children's League of Pity

 # HOUSTON MILL, East Linton   ♿
(Mr & Mrs Alastair Bell)
Attractive riverside cottage garden landscaped round historic mill, home of Andrew Meikle, inventor of the threshing machine in 1760 and mentor of civil engineer, John Rennie. This is a new garden created from a field in the last four years and includes large lawns, deep herbaceous borders, a shrub rose bank, camomile lawn and wild hedgerows. Beautiful riverbank willows. Riverside walks, horses and white Galloway cattle. Farmhouse teas. Plant stall. Visitors may park at nearby National Trust property, Preston Mill, and walk across bridge to garden. Also signposted on slip road off A1, through Phantassie farmyard and past NTS doocot to river. Children must be accompanied. Dogs on lead please.
Admission £1.50 Accompanied children & OAPs 50p
SUNDAY 5th JUNE 10 am – 6 pm
40% to World Wildlife Fund

INVERESK, near Musselburgh

Catherine Lodge	-	Mr Philip Mackenzie Ross
Oak Lodge	-	Mr & Mrs Michael Kennedy
Eskhill House	-	Robin & Lindsay Burley
Shepherd House	-	Sir Charles & Lady Fraser (see separate entry)
Inveresk Lodge	-	The National Trust for Scotland

Inveresk is a unique and unspoiled village on the southern fringes of Musselburgh. There have been settlements here since Roman times. The present houses mostly date from the late 17th and early 18th century. All have well laid out gardens enclosed by high stone walls. Each garden has its own individual character – some formal, some less so, some old, some new. They all contain a wide range of shrubs, trees and many interesting and unusual plants. Sale of needlework. Plant stall. Teas.
Admission £2.00 (includes all gardens) Accompanied children under 12 free.
SUNDAY 10th JULY 2 – 6 pm
40% to Haematology Ward, Royal Infirmary of Edinburgh

LENNOXLOVE, Haddington   ♿ (partly)
(Duke of Hamilton)
Lennoxlove, parts of which date back to the 14th century, houses the core of the famous Hamilton Palace collection of pictures, porcelain and furniture, also the death mask, casket and ring of Mary, Queen of Scots. The lime avenue, known as Politician's Walk, is where Secretary Maitland pondered the affairs of state during Queen Mary's reign. 17th century sundial by Gifford. The ancient keep is approached by way of a roundel of wild cherry trees containing a 40ft star of snowdrops, in the centre of which is an ash planted by Queen Elizabeth, the Queen Mother in 1967. The white Cadzow herd of wild cattle may be seen across the ha-ha. Plant stall. Tea room open: 10am – 5pm. Guided tours of house every 15 minutes 2pm – 5pm. Route: 1½ miles south of Haddington on B6369, 18 miles east of Edinburgh off A1.
Admission £1.00 Children 20p Guided tour of house £1.50
SUNDAY 15th MAY 10 am – 5 pm
40% to The Lennoxlove Trust

LUFFNESS, Aberlady   ♿ (weather permitting)
(Luffness Limited)
16th century castle with earlier foundations. Fruit garden built by Napoleonic prisoners-of-war. Tea in house. Plant stall. Donations please.
SUNDAY 26th JUNE 2 – 6 pm
40% to Scottish Society for the Prevention of Cruelty to Animals

---

SHEPHERD HOUSE, Inveresk, nr Musselburgh
(Sir Charles & Lady Fraser)
One acre, walled garden in 18th century village. Many interesting and unusual plants and shrubs. Old fashioned rose border with rose bower, herb garden, potager, formal pond and parterre. No teas or stalls.
Admission £1.00
THURSDAY 5th MAY – SUNDAY 8th MAY 2 – 5.30 pm. Exhibition of Botanical Paintings
THURSDAY 9th JUNE 2 – 5.30 pm
SUNDAY 10th JULY 2 – 6 pm (see under Inveresk opening), or by appointment.
40% to the Haematology Ward, Royal Infirmary of Edinburgh

STENTON VILLAGE GARDENS &. (some)
Stenton is a conservation village considered to be the best preserved in East Lothian. Several varied and interesting gardens in and around the village will be open. Teas and maps available in the Village Hall. Plant stall. A festival of flowers in Stenton Parish Church. Follow signs from A1 East Linton/Dunbar.
Admission £1.50 Children over 14 & OAPs £1.00
SUNDAY 22nd MAY 2 – 6 pm
40% to the Scottish Children's Hospice

TYNINGHAME, Dunbar &.
(Tyninghame Gardens Limited)
Splendid 17th century pink sandstone Scottish baronial house, remodelled in 1829 by William Burn, rises out of a sea of plants. Herbaceous border, formal rose garden, Lady Haddington's secret garden with old fashioned roses, formal walled garden with sculpture and yew hedges. The "wilderness" spring garden with magnificent rhododendrons, azaleas, flowering trees and bulbs. Grounds include quarter mile beech avenue to sea, famous "apple walk", Romanesque ruin of St Baldred's Church, views across parkland to Tyne estuary and Lammermuir Hills. Tyninghame 1 mile.
Admission £1.50 Children 75p
SUNDAY 29th MAY 2 – 6 pm
40% to Richard Cave Multiple Sclerosis Holiday Home, Leuchie

WINTON HOUSE, Pencaitland
(Sir David Ogilvy's 1968 Trust)
17th century Renaissance house. Decorative stone chimneys and dormers. William Wallace, master mason. Early 19th century castellated entrance. Beautiful plaster ceilings and stone carving, fine pictures and furniture. Masses of daffodils. Fine trees, terraced gardens. House conducted tour: £3.50, children under 14 £1.00. Tea and biscuits in house. From Pencaitland, lodge and wrought-iron gates two thirds of a mile on A6093, or, on B6355, archway and wrought-iron gates one mile from New Winton village, drive half a mile.
Admission £1.00 Children 25p
SUNDAY 17th APRIL 2 – 6 pm
40% to Royal Commonwealth Society for the Blind

EDINBURGH & WEST LOTHIAN
(LOTHIAN REGION)

Joint District Organisers: **Mrs J C Monteith,** 7 West Stanhope Place,
Edinburgh EH12 5HQ

Mrs Charles Welwood, Kirknewton House, Kirknewton,
West Lothian EH27 8DA

Joint Hon. Treasurers: **Mrs J C Monteith and Mrs Charles Welwood**

DATES OF OPENING

Dalmeny Park, South Queensferry .... Date to be announced

Newliston, Kirkliston .... Wednesdays to Sundays inclusive
4 May – 5 June   2 – 6pm

Dean Gardens & Ann Street, Edinburgh .... Sunday 10 April   2 – 6pm

Douglas Crescent Gardens, Edinburgh .... Saturday 23 April   2 – 5pm

Hethersett, Balerno .... Sunday 1 May   2 – 5.30pm

Colinton Gardens, Edinburgh .... Sunday 8 May   2 – 6pm

The Walled Garden Centre, Hopetoun House .... Sunday 15 May   1 – 5pm

Dr Neil's Garden, Duddingston .... Sat & Sun 21/22 May   2 – 5pm

Kirknewton House, Kirknewton .... Sun-Fri 5 – 10 June   2 – 6pm

Malleny House Garden, Balerno .... Sunday 12 June   2 – 5pm

Arthur Lodge, Dalkeith Road, Edinburgh .... Sat & Sun 18/19 June   2 – 5pm

Philpstoun House, Linlithgow .... Sunday 10 July   2 – 5.30pm

Suntrap Horticultural Centre, Edinburgh .... Sunday 7 August   2.30 – 5pm

South Queensferry & Dalmeny .... Sunday 14 August   2 – 6pm

Dr Neil's Garden, Duddingston .... Sat & Sun 20/21 August   2 – 5pm

Belgrave Crescent Gardens, Edinburgh .... Sunday 21 August   2 – 5pm

ARTHUR LODGE, 60 Dalkeith Road, Edinburgh ♿
(Mr S R Friden)
Formal herbaceous garden. Sunken Italian garden and White garden. Plant stall. Teas.
Entrance to garden in Blacket Place, opposite the Commonwealth Pool.
Admission £1.00 Children 60p
SATURDAY & SUNDAY 18th & 19th JUNE 2 – 5pm
40% to Cockburn Association (Pinkerton Fund)

BELGRAVE CRESCENT GARDENS, Edinburgh ♿
(Belgrave Crescent Proprietors)
Central city garden with lawns and trees, shrubs and flowers and paths leading down to
the Water of Leith and a waterfall. Route: first left over Dean Bridge out of Edinburgh.
Admission £1.00 Children & Senior Citizens 50p
SUNDAY 21st AUGUST 2 – 5 pm
40% to King George's Fund for Sailors

COLINTON GARDENS, Edinburgh
MILLHOLME, Grant Avenue (Mr Cecil Mcgregor)
Rhododendrons, shrubs and rock garden. From village, proceed up Woodhall Road,
second left turn, then first right (Grant Avenue) entrance on right.
MOUNT PLEASANT, 5 Castlelaw Road (Mr William Alexander)
Spring flowering shrubs, rhododendrons, camellias. Car park free. Mount Pleasant is 70
yards up Castlelaw Road.
Admission £1.00 Children under 8 free
SUNDAY 8th MAY 2 – 6 pm
40% to The Order of St Lazarus Charitable Fund

DALMENY PARK, South Queensferry
(The Earl of Rosebery)
Acres of snowdrops on Mons Hill. Cars free. Teas available in the Courtyard Restaurant,
Dalmeny House. Route: South Queensferry, off A90 road to B924. Pedestrians and cars
enter by Leuchold Gate and exit by Chapel Gate.
Admission £1.00 Children under 14 free
Date to be announced
40% to St Columba's Hospice

DEAN GARDENS & ANN STREET, Edinburgh
DEAN GARDENS (Dean Gardens Committee of Management)
Privately owned town gardens on north bank of the Water of Leith. 13½ acres of spring
bulbs, daffodils, trees and shrubs and other interesting features. Entrance at Ann Streeet
or Eton Terrace.
ANN STREET GARDENS
Ann Street is one of the few Georgian streets where the houses on both sides boast their
own front gardens. They are particularly pretty in spring and early summer with
flowering trees, shrubs and bulbs.
Admission to both gardens £1.00 Children 50p
SUNDAY 10th APRIL 2 – 6 pm
40% to QNI (Scotland) and the Gardens Fund of the National Trust for Scotland

DOUGLAS CRESCENT GARDENS, Edinburgh

Woodland sloping to Water of Leith, about 3 acres, with level lawns and shrubs, etc. at east end. Daffodils.

Admission £1.00 Children & OAPs 50p

SATURDAY 23rd APRIL 2 – 5 pm

40% to The Woodland Trust

DR NEIL'S GARDEN, Duddingston Village

(Drs Andrew & Nancy Neil)

Landscaped garden on the lower slopes of Arthur's Seat using conifers, heathers and alpines. Teas in Kirk Hall. Plant stalls.

Admission £1.00 Children free

SATURDAY & SUNDAY 21st & 22nd MAY 2 – 5 pm

SATURDAY & SUNDAY 20th & 21st AUGUST 2 – 5 pm

All takings to Scotland's Gardens Scheme

HETHERSETT, Balerno

(Professor & Mrs I G Stewart)

Informal, woodland garden with daffodils, primulas and rhododendrons. No dogs, please. Plant stall. Route: On A70, half mile beyond Balerno turning.

Admission £1.00 Children 50p

SUNDAY 1st MAY 2 – 5.30 pm

20% to Barnardo's, 20% to Riding for the Disabled

KIRKNEWTON HOUSE, Kirknewton &

(Mr & Mrs Charles Welwood)

Extensive woodland garden. Rhododendrons, azaleas and shrubs. Plant stall. Route: Either A71 or A70 on to B7031.

Admission £1.00 Children 50p

SUNDAY 5th- FRIDAY 10th JUNE 2 – 6 pm (Teas on Sunday only)

40% to St Columba's Hospice

MALLENY HOUSE GARDEN, Balerno &

(The National Trust for Scotland)

A two acre walled garden with 17th century clipped yew trees, lawns and borders. Wide and varied selection of herbaceous plants and shrubs. Shrub roses including NCCPG. 19th century rose collection. Ornamental vegetable and herb garden. Greenhouse display. Georgian wing, Malleny House open. Scottish National Bonsai Collection. Plant stall. Tea and biscuits. In Balerno, off Lanark Road West (A70) 7 miles from Edinburgh city centre. Buses: Lothian 43, Eastern Scottish, 66 & 44.

Admission £1.00 Children & OAPs 50p

SUNDAY 12th JUNE 2 – 5 pm

40% to NTS Threave Bursary Fund

For other opening details see page 141

NEWLISTON, Kirkliston &

(Mr J S Findlay)

18th century designed landscape. Rhododendrons and azaleas. The house, which was designed by Robert Adam, is open and a collection of costumes will be on display. Teas. On Sundays tea is in the Edinburgh Cookery School which operates in the William Adam Coach House. Also on Sundays there is a ride-on steam model railway from 2 – 5 pm. Four miles from Forth Road Bridge, entrance off B800.

Admission to House & Garden £1 Children & OAPs 50p

WEDNESDAYS – SUNDAYS inclusive each week from 4th MAY to 5th JUNE 2 – 6pm

40% to King George V Fund for Sailors

PHILPSTOUN HOUSE, Linlithgow &

(Mr & Mrs Dermot Jenkinson)

17th century house (not open, except for tea). Cake and candy. Light refreshments. Pony rides, weather permitting. A904 from Forth Bridge roundabout. Lodge is on right $\frac{1}{4}$ mile after Abercorn School.

Admission £1.00 Children under 7 free

SUNDAY 10th JULY 2 – 5.30 pm

40% to Save the Children Fund

SOUTH QUEENSFERRY & DALMENY

Around twelve small gardens in varied styles – cottage, water, plantsman's, bedding. Teas. Tickets and maps available from Dalmeny Kirk Hall.

Inclusive admission £1.50 Accompanied children free OAPs £1.00

SUNDAY 14th AUGUST 2 – 6 pm

40% to RNLI, South Queensferry

SUNTRAP HORTICULTURAL & GARDENING CENTRE 43 Gogarbank, Edinburgh &

(Oatridge Agricultural College)

Suntrap is a horticultural out-centre of Oatridge Agricultural College. A compact garden of 1.7 hectares it includes rock and water features, peat walls, sunken garden, woodland plantings and glasshouse area. The garden provides facilities for professional and amateur instruction, horticultural advice and a place to visit. Refreshments. Plant sales. Exhibits. No charge for cars. Route: Half a mile west of Edinburgh bypass roundabout, off A8. Bus route:Eastern Scottish 37. Open daily throughout the year 9.00 am – 4.30 pm.

Admission £1.00 Children & OAPs 50p

SUNDAY 7th AUGUST 2.30 – 5pm

40% to Gardeners' Royal Benevolent Society (Netherbyres Appeal)

THE WALLED GARDEN CENTRE, Hopetoun House &

(Mr & Mrs Dougal Philip)

Guided tours around the Walled Garden exploring the different design themes and huge range of plants you could use in your garden; all-seasons mixed border, exciting and calm borders, oriental garden, colour-themed flower garden, grass garden, woodland walk, Buddleia Bank dry and sunny, alpine frames. South Queensferry 2 miles, Newton village three-quarters of a mile, Edinburgh 12 miles. Follow signs to Hopetoun House.

Admission by collection box and raffle

SUNDAY 15th MAY 1 – 5 pm

All proceeds to Scotland's Gardens Scheme

ETTRICK & LAUDERDALE
(BORDERS REGION)

Joint District Organisers: **Mrs M Shaw-Stewart,** Linthill, Lilliesleaf TD6 9HU
Mrs Gavin Younger, Chapel-on-Leader, Earlston TD4 6AW

Hon. Treasurer: **Mr D Wilson,** Royal Bank of Scotland, St Dunstan's High Street, Melrose TD6 9PF

DATES OF OPENING

Bemersyde, Melrose	Sunday 24 April	2 – 6pm
Allerly Mains & Hollybank, Gattonside	Sunday 29 May	2 – 5.30pm
Chapel-on-Leader, Earlston	Sunday 12 June	2 – 6pm
Midlem Village	Sunday 19 June	2 – 6pm
Linthill, Lilliesleaf & **Shawburn,** Midlem	Sunday 3 July	2 – 5.30pm
Mellerstain, Gordon	Sunday 17 July	12.30 – 6.30pm
Abbotsford, Melrose	Sunday 7 August	2 – 5.30pm

ABBOTSFORD, Melrose ♿ (partly)

(Mrs P Maxwell-Scott, OBE)

House and garden built and laid out by Sir Walter Scott, who built the house 1812 – 1832 when he died. Herbaceous and annual borders. Teashop in grounds. Jedburgh Branch British Legion Pipe Band. Admission price is to garden only. To house and garden £2.60, children £1.30. Bus party – adults £2.00, children £1.10. Melrose 2 miles; Galashiels 1½ miles.

Admission £1.50

SUNDAY 7th AUGUST 2 – 5.30 pm

40% to British Red Cross Society

ALLERLY MAINS, Gattonside, Melrose

(Mr & Mrs J N Rutherford)

Garden started in 1989. Terraced on hillside facing south, spectacular view to Tweed – Eildon Hills. Teas. Gattonside: 2 miles from Leaderfoot Bridge A68, north side of Tweed.

JOINT OPENING WITH HOLLYBANK

Admission 50p Children free

SUNDAY 29th MAY 2 – 5.30 pm

40% to Cancer Research

BEMERSYDE, Melrose ♿

(The Earl Haig)

16th century peel tower reconstructed in the 17th century with added mansion house. Garden laid out by Field Marshal Earl Haig. Views of Eildon Hills. Woodland walks. Admission to garden only. St Boswells via Clintmains or Melrose via Leaderfoot Bridge.

Admission £1.65 Children under 10 free

SUNDAY 24th APRIL 2 – 6 pm

40% to Lady Haig's Poppy Factory

CHAPEL-ON-LEADER, Earlston ♿

(Mr & Mrs Gavin Younger)

Large country garden with lovely views of park and river. Inspired by Sissinghurst and Jekyll, planting is informal with interesting foliage as well as flowers. Divided into different areas there is a white garden, rose avenue, azalea border, mixed borders with old fashioned roses, clematis and rose covered pergolas, paved swimming pool area, recently restored water and bog garden, woodland and rhododendron walks and a large walled kitchen garden. Home made teas. Turn off A68 at sign 2 miles north of Earlston, 4 miles south of Lauder.

Admission £1.50 Children free

SUNDAY 12th JUNE 2 – 6 pm

40% to Save the Children Fund

 # HOLLYBANK, Bakers Road, Gattonside

(Lady Stewart)

Shrub roses, ericaceous border, rockery. Small woodland garden. Teas at Allerly Mains. Plant stall. Galashiels/Gattonside road (B6360) at Lowood Bridge or Leaderfoot/Gattonside road (B6360) off A68.

JOINT OPENING WITH ALLERLY MAINS.

Admission £1.00 Children over 5 & OAPs 50p

SUNDAY 29th MAY 2 – 5.30 p.m.

40% to Scottish Motor Neurone Disease Association

LINTHILL, Lilliesleaf &

(Mr & Mrs Michael Shaw Stewart)
Shrub and rose garden around house. Ponds, riverside and woodland walks. Walled garden. Lilliesleaf nursery (commercial) plant stall. Teas in house. One mile from Lilliesleaf.
JOINT OPENING WITH SHAWBURN (½ mile).
Admission £1.00 Children under 5 free
SUNDAY 3rd JULY 2 – 5.30 p.m.
40% to Barnardo's

MELLERSTAIN, Gordon &

(The Earl of Haddington)
Adam mansion with formal terrace and rose garden. Extensive grounds with lake and many fine trees. Tearoom in grounds. House open 12.30 – 5 pm; last admission 4.30 pm. Admission to House and Garden £3.50, OAPs £3.00, Children £1.50. Route: Gordon, 3 miles on A6089 or at turn off A6105 from A68 at Earlston 6 miles, both signposted Mellerstain House.
Admission £1.50
SUNDAY 17th JULY 12.30 – 6.30 pm
Donation to Scotland's Gardens Scheme

MIDLEM VILLAGE, near Selkirk

Ashby Cottage	- Mr & Mrs A Scott	**Croft Cottage**	- Mrs Williams (Plant stall)
The Old Manse	- Cmdr & Mrs Bulman	**Rose Cottage**	- Mr & Mrs Dickson
Sunny Brae	- Mr & Mrs MacKay	**The Cottage**	- Mr & Mrs Pavey
Linden Lea	- Mrs Conway	**Fernbank**	- Mr & Mrs Hunter
Cheviot View	- Mr & Mrs Mitchell	**Wellbrae**	- Mr & Mrs Skinner

A number of small gardens in picturesque village. Each garden entirely different with something of interest for everyone. Some rare plants. Plant stall. Home baked teas in Village Hall. Tickets to be bought outside Village Hall. Midlem is 4 miles from Selkirk, 4 miles south of Melrose, 2 miles north of Lilliesleaf.
Admission £1.00 includes all gardens. Children & OAPs 50p
SUNDAY 19th JUNE 2 – 6 p.m.
30% to British Red Cross Society
10% to Village Hall

SHAWBURN, Midlem &

(Mr & Mrs C C Allan)
Recently made small garden with assortment of interesting plants. Three-quarters of a mile south east of Midlem.
JOINT OPENING WITH LINTHILL (½ mile).
Admission £1.00 Children under 5 free
SUNDAY 3rd JULY 2 – 5.30 p.m.
40% to Riding for the Disabled Association (Borders branch)

FIFE
(FIFE REGION)

District Organiser: **Mrs David L Skinner**, Lathrisk House, Freuchie KY7 7HX

Area Organisers: **Mrs James Barr,** Burnbank, Drumhead, Saline KY12 9LL
Mrs Christine Gordon, The Tannery, Kilconquhar,
Leven KY9 1LQ
Mrs Roderick F Jones, Nether Kinneddar, Saline KY12 9LJ
Mrs N Stewart-Meiklejohn, 6 Howard Place,
St Andrews KY16 9HL
Mrs Robert Turcan, Lindores House, Cupar KY14 6JD

Hon. Treasurer: **Mrs A B Cran,** Karbet, Freuchie KY7 7EY

DATES OF OPENING

Cambo House, Kingsbarns	Daily all year 10am – 4pm	
Cambo House, Kingsbarns	Sunday 27 February (provisionally)	2 – 5pm
Cambo House, Kingsbarns	Sunday 10 April	2 – 5pm
The Murrel, Aberdour	Sunday 24 April	10am – 5pm
Whitehill, Aberdour	Sunday 8 May	2 – 5.30pm
Birkhill, Cupar	Sunday 15 May	2.30 – 6pm
Micklegarth, Aberdour	Sunday 15 May	2 – 5.30pm
Earlshall Castle, Leuchars	Sunday 22 May	2 – 6pm
Kirklands House, Saline	Sunday 5 June	2 – 5.30pm
Falkland Palace Garden	Sunday 5 June	2 – 5pm
Gilston, Largoward	Sunday 12 June	1.30 – 6pm
The Murrel, Aberdour	Sunday 12 June	10am – 5pm
Balcaskie, Pittenweem	Sunday 19 June	2 – 6pm
Lathrisk, Freuchie	Sunday 19 June	2 – 5.30pm
Kellie Castle, Pittenweem	Sunday 26 June	11am – 5pm
Myres Castle, Auchtermuchty	Sunday 26 June	2 – 5pm
Hillside, Ceres	Sunday 3 July	2 – 5.30pm
St Andrews Botanic Garden	Sunday 3 July	10am – 6pm
Hill of Tarvit, Cupar	Sunday 10 July	11am – 5pm
Crail Gardens	Sat & Sun 23/24 July	2 – 6pm
Hilton House, Cupar	Sunday 24 July	2.30 – 5.30pm
Falkland Palace Garden	Sunday 7 August	2 – 5pm
Micklegarth, Aberdour	Sunday 7 August	2 – 5.30pm
Pittenweem Gardens	Sat & Sun 13/14 August	2 – 5.30pm
The Murrel, Aberdour	Sunday 11 September	10am – 5pm
The Murrel, Aberdour	Sunday 18 September	10am – 5pm
Hill of Tarvit Plant Sale	Saturday 1 October	10.30am – 4pm
	Sunday 2 October	2 – 5pm

BALCASKIE, Pittenweem ♿ (top terrace only)
(Sir Ralph Anstruther of that Ilk Bt.)
There has been a house, originally fortified, at Balcaskie since the 13th century and a charter granted to Ivor Cook by King Alexander III in 1223 exists. In 1665 Sir William Bruce altered the castle, laid out the terraces and made what he called "the first mansion house in Scotland". He lived there before building, and moving to, Kinross House. The Anstruther family acquired the property in 1698. Tea and biscuits. National Trust stall. East Neuk Pipe Band. Route: A917, 2 miles from Anstruther. Enter by Lodge gate. Admission £1.70 Children free.
SUNDAY 19th JUNE 2 – 6 pm
40% to S.S.A.F.A.

BIRKHILL, Cupar ♿
(The Earl & Countess of Dundee)
Victorian baronial house. Traditional walled garden. Wild woodland garden, a dream in the spring. Beach and cliff walks. Home baked cream teas. Plant and home produce stalls. Location 2 miles west of Balmerino, off A94.
Also two charming cottage gardens, one an alpine garden, by kind permission of Mr & Mrs Brownfather and Mr & Mrs Lumsden.
Admission £2.00 Children free
SUNDAY 15th MAY 2.30 – 6 pm
40% to Luthrie School

CAMBO HOUSE, Kingsbarns ♿
(Mr & Mrs T P N Erskine)
A charming and romantic garden designed around the Cambo burn, with a small waterfall spanned by an oriental bridge set against a weeping willow. It is a traditional walled garden serving the superb Victorian Mansion House (not open) with flowers, fruit and vegetables. The garden retains many original features with recently restored greeenhouses and clipped box hedges. There is also a woodland walk along the burn. Many rare and unusual plants. Always something of interest. The season starts early with acres of snowdrops and snowflakes. Masses of daffodils and other spring bulbs. Chrysanthemums and dahlias in early autumn and lovely autumn colours. Teas, stalls and plant stall at special openings. Cars free. Dogs on lead please. Route: A917
Admission £2.00 Children free
OPEN ALL YEAR ROUND 10 am – 4 pm
SNOWDROP DAY – Provisionally SUNDAY 27th FEBRUARY 2 – 5 pm
40% to Alzheimer's Scotland, Fife Project
DAFFODIL DAY – SUNDAY 10th APRIL 2 – 5 pm
40% to British Diabetic Association, Fife Branch

CRAIL: SMALL GARDENS IN THE BURGH
(The Gardeners of Crail)
A number of small gardens in varied styles: cottage, historic, plantsman's, bedding. Exhibition of paintings at Lobster Cottage, Shoregate. Exhibition of Scottish contemporary metalwork by members of the British Artist Blacksmiths' Association. Approach Crail from either St Andrews or Anstruther, A917. Park in the Marketgait. Tickets and map available only from Mrs Auchinleck, 2 Castle Street, Crail. Admission £2.00 Acccompanied Children free OAPs £1.00
SATURDAY & SUNDAY 23rd and 24th JULY 2 – 6 pm
20% to Fife Macmillan Project (Hospice)
20% to Crail Preservation Society

EARLSHALL CASTLE, Leuchars   &

(The Baron & Baroness of Earlshall)
Walled gardens designed by Sir Robert Lorimer. Yew topiary, herbaceous borders, bowling green, rose terrace, orchard, secret garden, pleached limes, espaliererd fruit trees. Herb garden saved from serious decline over last seven years. No dogs in garden please. Woodland walk, gift shop. Plant stall. Home baked teas in Lorimer Tea Room. Route: A919. Leuchars, Cupar 8 miles, St Andrews 6 miles.
Admission: House & Garden £2.00 Children free
SUNDAY 22nd MAY 2 – 6 pm
40% to Sense (Scotland)

FALKLAND PALACE GARDEN, Falkland   &

(The National Trust for Scotland)
The Palace was the hunting seat of the Stewart monarchs during the 15th and 16th centuries. The present garden was laid out after the last war on the site of the original Royal Garden and contains a Royal Tennis Court built in 1539 and in play today. Tearooms nearby in village. Free car park. Admission to Palace and garden £4.00. Children & OAPs £2.00. Route: A912.
Admission £2.00 Children £1.00
SUNDAY 5th JUNE and SUNDAY 7th AUGUST 2 – 5 pm
40% to NTS Threave Bursary Fund
For other opening details see page 134

GILSTON, Largoward

(Mr & Mrs Edward Baxter)
Late 18th century house with informal and wild gardens, primulas, meconopsis, rhododendrons and azaleas. Herbaceous and shrub borders. Pony rides. Wildflower meadow and butterflies. National Trust for Scotland and plant stalls. Home baked teas. 8 miles from St Andrews, 6 miles from Leven on A915.
Admission £2.00 Accompanied children free
SUNDAY 12th JUNE 1.30 – 6 pm
40% to Equine Grass Sickness

HILL OF TARVIT, Cupar

(The National Trust for Scotland)
Charming Edwardian mansion house designed in 1906 by Sir Robert Lorimer for jute magnate, Mr F B Sharp. Contains his fine collection of furniture, paintings, tapestries and Chinese porcelain. The house stands in beautiful grounds with many interesting and unusual plants, shrubs and trees. Heathers, heaths, rose garden and delightful woodland walk to toposcope. Admission to house and garden: £3.00, children and OAPs £1.50. Perfect place for a picnic. Tearoom. Plant stall. Route A916.
Admission to Garden: £1.00 Children 50p
SUNDAY 10th JULY 11 am – 5 pm
40% to NTS Threave Bursary Fund
SCOTLAND'S GARDENS SCHEME PLANT SALE
Bring plants, buy plants. Large variety of shrubs and big clumps of herbaceous plants at bargain prices. Saturday—Coffee and snack lunches. Sunday—Teas.
SATURDAY 1st OCTOBER 10.30 am – 4 pm
SUNDAY 2nd OCTOBER 2 – 5 pm
40% to East Fife Members Centre of National Trust for Scotland
For other opening details see page 135

HILLSIDE, Ceres &

(Mrs Rachel Peterkin)

A mixed garden in $3\frac{1}{2}$ acres with trees, shrubs, heathers, dwarf conifers, herbaceous and rock plants. A woodland and secret garden. Plant stall. Teas. Entrance at 30 mph limit sign on Cupar/Ceres road.

Admission £1.50 Children 50p OAPs £1.00

SUNDAY 3rd JULY 2 – 5.30 pm

40% to Fife Folk Museum

HILTON HOUSE, Cupar

(Mrs M M Wilson)

Walled garden, roses and herbaceous. Woodland walk. Stalls. Cream teas. One mile north of Cupar passing Adamson Hospital.

Admission £1.50 Children under 12 free

SUNDAY 24th JULY 2.30 – 5.30 pm

40% to local charities

KELLIE CASTLE, Pittenweem &

(The National Trust for Scotland)

The oldest part of the castle dates from about 1360. The building, mainly 16th and 17th century probably assumed its present dimensions about 1606. Kellie is a very fine example of the domestic architecture of lowland Scotland. Virtually abandoned in the early 19th century, the castle was leased to, and restored by, Professor James Lorimer from 1876. Includes Lorimer exhibition and children's nursery. Walled organic garden features box edged paths, rose arches, herbaceous plants and shrub roses. Admission to house and garden £3.00, children £1.50. Tearoom within castle available to those visiting garden only. Adventure playground. Good picnic area.

Admission £1.00 Children & OAPs 50p

SUNDAY 26th JUNE 11 am – 5 pm

40% to NTS Threave Bursary Fund

For further opening details see page 137

KIRKLANDS HOUSE, Saline

(Mr & Mrs Peter Hart)

Large garden with herbaceous borders and woodland walks. Teas. Plant stall. Ample parking in village by bus shelter.

Admission £1.50

SUNDAY 5th JUNE 2 – 5.30 pm

40% to National Asthma Campaign

LATHRISK HOUSE and OLD LATHRISK, Freuchie &

(Mr & Mrs David Skinner and Mr & Mrs David Wood)

Herbaceous borders, shrubs, lawns and mature trees in beautiful setting with views over the Howe of Fife and the East Lomond. Teas. Cake and produce stall. Plant stall.

Admission £1.50 Children free

SUNDAY 19th JUNE 2 – 5.30 pm

40% to Falkland Parish Church

MICKLEGARTH, Aberdour &

(Gordon and Kathleen Maxwell)
Small, informal garden with shrubbery, herbaceous and island beds and rock garden. Teas. Plant stall. In heart of historic seaside village. Route: A921. Train, bus or car to Aberdour, park in car park at railway station; proceed west along High Street approximately 200 metres.
Admission £1.00 Children 25p OAPs 50p
SUNDAY 15th MAY 2 – 5.30 pm.
40% to R.N.L.I.
SUNDAY 7th AUGUST 2 – 5.30 pm.
40% to Save the Children Fund

MYRES CASTLE, Auchtermuchty &

(Captain David Fairlie of Myres)
Fortified house, with 18th century additions, built in 1530 by John Scrymgeour, Master of the King's Works, who completed Falkland Palace for James V in 1542. Woodland gardens with pond. Layout of walled garden based on one of the Vatican gardens. Yew hedges form "garden rooms" for flowering shrubs. Beds of shrub, hybrid roses and herbaceous plants and lupins. Plant stall. Home baked teas under cover. A chance to meet the Scouts in Camp. Cars free. 1/4 mile south of Auchtermuchty on A983 road to Falkland. Perth/Kirkcaldy buses stop at Myres Castle lodge. 100 yards walk to garden.
Admission £2.00 Children free OAPs £1.00
SUNDAY 26th JUNE 2 – 5 pm
40% Cupar District Scouts

PITTENWEEM: SMALL GARDENS IN THE BURGH

(The Gardeners of Pittenweem)
A good number of small gardens in varied styles, hidden in the streets and wynds of this beautiful and rather secrtive burgh. Two excellent tea rooms in High Street. Many exhibitions of contemporary art running concurrently with garden openings. Festival in village starts 7th August. Nice dogs welcome. Tickets and map available only from Mrs M G Williamson, Priorsgait, 15 Cove Wynd. Route: A917.
Admission £2.00 Accompanied children free OAPs £1.00
SATURDAY & SUNDAY 13th & 14th AUGUST 2 – 5.30 pm
40% to R.N.L.I. and Pittenweem Festival

ST ANDREWS BOTANIC GARDEN, Canongate, St Andrews &

(North East Fife District Council)
Peat, rock and water gardens. Tree, shrub, bulb and herbaceous borders. Large range of plants. Plant stall. Route: A915. Well signposted in St Andrews.
Admission £1.00 Accompanied children 50p
SUNDAY 3rd JULY 10 am – 6 pm
40% to Friends of the Botanic Garden

THE MURREL, Aberdour
(Mr John E Milne)
Many rare and unusual plants not often found growing in Scotland, this garden is worth a visit throughout the season as there is always something new to see. Features: spring bulbs, shrubs, rhododendrons, roses (including shrub roses), rockeries, walled garden and woodland walks. Tea and biscuits. Plant stall selling only plants seen growing in the garden. House not open. Garden not suitable for wheelchairs. No dogs please. On B9157 Inverkeithing/Kirkcaldy road, opposite Croftgarry Farm.
Admission £1.00
SUNDAYS 24th APRIL, 12th JUNE, 11th & 18th SEPTEMBER 10 am – 5 pm
40% to Royal Sick Children's Hospital, Edinburgh

WHITEHILL, Aberdour &
(Mr & Mrs Gavin Reed)
Shrubs and specie rhododendrons, a fine collection of interesting trees and a new lochan. Teas. Good plant stall. Route: B9157.
Admission £1.00
SUNDAY 8th MAY 2 – 5.30 pm
40% to Royal Blind Asylum and School

ISLE OF ARRAN
(STRATHCLYDE REGION)

District Organiser: **Mrs S C Gibbs,** Dougarie, Isle of Arran KA27 8EB

Hon. Treasurer: **Mr J Hill,** Bank of Scotland, Brodick, Isle of Arran KA27 8AL

DATES OF OPENING

Strabane, Brodick .... Sunday 1 May	2 – 5pm
Dougarie. .... Sunday 26 June	2 – 6pm
Brodick Castle & Country Park .... Wednesday 6th July	10am – 5pm
Brodick Castle & Country Park .... Wednesday 3rd August	10am – 5pm

---

BRODICK CASTLE & COUNTRY PARK 👤 (mostly)
(The National Trust for Scotland & Cunninghame District Council)
Semi-tropical plants and shrubs. Walled garden. Rock garden. Free guided walks. Car park free. Morning coffee, lunch and tea available in Castle. NTS shop. Brodick 2 miles. Service buses from Brodick Pier to Castle. Regular sailings from Ardrossan and from Claonaig (Argyll). Information from Caledonian MacBrayne, Gourock. Tel: 0475 33755.
Admission to Garden & Country Park £2.00. Children & OAPs £1.00
WEDNESDAYS 6th JULY and 3rd AUGUST 10 a.m. – 5 p.m.
40% to NTS Threave Bursary Fund
For other opening details see page 131

DOUGARIE
(Mr & Mrs S C Gibbs)
Terraced garden in castellated folly. Shrubs, herbaceous borders, traditional kitchen garden. Tea. Produce stall. Blackwaterfoot 5 miles. Regular ferry sailing from Ardrossan and from Claonaig (Argyll). Information from Caledonian MacBrayne, Gourock. Tel: 0475 33755.
Admission £1.00 Children 50p
SUNDAY 26th JUNE 2 – 6 pm
40% to Episcopalian Church, Isle of Arran

 # STRABANE, Brodick
(Lady Jean Fforde)
Woodland garden. Azaleas, rhododendrons, cherries and daffodils. Teas. Stall. Car park free. One mile from Brodick on A841 to Corrie. Regular sailings from Ardrossan and Claonaig (Argyll). Information from Caledonian MacBrayne, Gourock. Tel: 0475 33755.
Admission £1.00 Children 50p
SUNDAY 1st MAY 2 – 5 p.m.
40% to Arran Lifeline

KINCARDINE & DEESIDE
(GRAMPIAN REGION)

District Organiser: **Mrs J Mackie,** Bent, Laurencekirk AB30 1EA

Area Organisers: **The Hon Mrs J K O Arbuthnott,** Kilternan, Arbuthnott, Laurencekirk AB30 1NA

Mrs E H Hartwell, Burnigill, Burnside, Fettercairn AB30 1XX

Hon. Treasurer: **Mr D S Gauld,** Clydesdale Bank, 24 High Street, Laurencekirk, Kincardine AB30 1AB

DATES OF OPENING

Shooting Greens, Strachan .... 25 April – 15 May by arrangement

Shooting Greens, Strachan .... Sunday 24 April	2 – 5pm
The Burn House & The Burn Garden House, Glenesk .... Sunday 29 May	2 – 5pm
Crathes Castle, Banchory .... Sunday 26 June	2 – 5pm
Bent, Laurencekirk .... Sunday 3 July	2 – 5pm
Drum Castle, Drumoak .... Sunday 10 July	2 – 5pm
Arbuthnott House, Laurencekirk .... Sunday 17 July	2 – 5pm
Bogarn & House of Strachan, Strachan .... Sunday 17 July	2 – 5pm
Douneside House, Tarland .... Sunday 24 July	2 – 6pm
Glenbervie House, Drumlithie .... Sunday 24 July	2 – 5pm
Balmanno, Marykirk .... Sunday 31 July	2 – 5.30pm

ARBUTHNOTT HOUSE, Laurencekirk

(The Viscount of Arbuthnott, CBE DSC)

17th century formal garden on unusually steep slope with grass terraces, herbaceous borders, shrubs, etc. Tea and biscuits. Plant stall. Route: between A92 and A94 on B967. Admission (Garden & car park) £1.50 Children & OAPs 80p

SUNDAY 17th JULY 2 – 5 pm

40% to Arbuthnott Parish Church

BALMANNO, Marykirk, by Laurencekirk

(Mr & Mrs Ronald Simson)

A traditional Scottish 18th century walled garden with flower borders and vegetable plots. Splendid views of the Grampians across the valley. Home baked teas. Plant stall. Route: Balmanno is three-quarters of a mile north of Marykirk, south of Laurencekirk on A937. Turn right at unmarked crossroads, up hill a few hundred yards on right. Admission £1.00 Children 50p

SUNDAY 31st JULY 2 – 5.30 p.m.

40% to Marykirk Village Hall Rebuilding Fund

BENT, Laurencekirk

(Mrs James Mackie)

Herbaceous borders, shrub border, woodland area and small White Garden. Large collection of plants, many interesting and unusual. Good plant and produce stall. Teas with home baking. Cars free. Route: 2½ miles from Laurencekirk on B9120 to Fettercairn. Admission £1.00 Children 50p

SUNDAY 3rd JULY 2 – 5 pm

40% to R.N.L.I.

BOGARN, Strachan, Banchory

(Mr & Mrs F H Hartley)

One acre garden started in 1985 in poor soil on rocks. Pond. Plant stall. Oils, watercolours, pastels, etc. for sale. Teas at House of Strachan. 2 miles from Strachan on B974 to Fettercairn, on left.

JOINT OPENING WITH HOUSE OF STRACHAN.

Admission £1.00 includes both gardens

SUNDAY 17th JULY 2 – 5 pm

20% to Glen o' Dee Hospital, Banchory
20% to Population Concern

CRATHES CASTLE, Banchory &

(The National Trust for Scotland)

Richly decorated tower house of the north eastern school built by the family of Burnett of Leys between 1553 – 96. Good examples of painted ceilings, fine furniture and interesting portraits. Walled gardens (3.75 acres) containing eight distinct and separate gardens, including magnificent yew hedges planted in 1702, rare shrubs and fine herbaceous borders. All combine to form the finest patterned garden in northern Scotland. Extensive wild gardens and grounds containing adventure playground, picnic areas and some 15 miles of marked trails. Exhibitions, shop and licensed restaurant (Taste of Scotland). Sale of plants, garden walks, ranger walks. Situated off A93 3 miles east of Banchory. Admission quoted includes castle, garden, estate and use of all facilities. Admission (combined ticket) £4.00 Children & OAPs £2.00

SUNDAY 26th JUNE 2 – 5 pm

40% to NTS Threave Bursary Fund
For other opening details see page 132

DOUNESIDE HOUSE, Tarland &

(The MacRobert Trusts)
Ornamental and rose gardens around a large lawn with uninterrupted views to the
Deeside Hills and Grampians; large, well-stocked vegetable garden, beech walks and
water gardens. Cars free. Tea in house. Plant stall. Towie and District Pipe Band. Tarland
1½ mile. Route: B9119 towards Aberdeen.
Admission £1.00 Children & OAPs 50p
SUNDAY 24th JULY 2 – 6 pm
40% to Queen's Nursing Institute (Scotland)

DRUM CASTLE, Drumoak, by Banchory &

(The National Trust for Scotland)
Walled garden of historic roses, opened June 1991. Roses representing 17th to 20th
centuries. Grounds contain arboretum, woodland walk, picnic area and farmland walk.
Marquee teas. Band. Plant sales. Admission to House £2. Drum Castle is 10 miles west of
Aberdeen and 8 miles east of Banchory on A93.
Admission £1.00 Children 50p
SUNDAY 10th JULY 2 – 5 pm
40% to NTS Threave Bursary Fund
For further details see page 141

GLENBERVIE HOUSE, Drumlithie, Stonehaven

(Mrs C S Macphie)
Nucleus of present day house dates from the 15th century. Additions in 17th and 19th
centuries. Walled garden with fine herbaceous and annual borders. Ornamental
conservatory contains a dazzling display of interesting plants, also woodland garden.
Teas. Plant stall. Cars free. Drumlithie 1 mile. Garden 1½ miles off A94. NOT SUITABLE
FOR WHEELCHAIRS.
Admission £1.50 Children 80p
SUNDAY 24th JULY 2 – 5 pm
40% to Kidney Research

HOUSE OF STRACHAN, Strachan, Banchory

(Dr & Mrs Colin McCance)
A mature garden of two acres, the grounds of what was Strachan Manse. It slopes south
to the River Feugh and has a variety of roses, herbaceous borders, heathers and other
plants and shrubs. Plant stall at Bogarn. Teas. On B976 on south side in centre of village
of Strachan.
JOINT OPENING WITH BOGARN.
Admission £1.00 includes both gardens.
SUNDAY 17th JULY 2 – 5 pm
20% to Glen o' Dee Hospital, Banchory
20% to Population Concern

SHOOTING GREENS, Strachan, Banchory ♿ (limited access)
(Mr & Mrs Donald Stuart-Hamilton)
Medium sized garden, landscaped with local stone, stems from terracing rough moorland near a burn and woodland glen. Short vistas and distant Grampian hills back raised, mixed, erica and alpine beds. Follies include Troll's Den, a row of cairns and small amphitheatre. Beyond a small orchard, sloping to ponds, lie short walks by burn and through mixed and beech groves, one to a view point. Forestry Commission walks nearby. CARS PLEASE PARK ALONG PUBLIC ROAD. Route: On east side, near top of north-south Deeside link road between Potarch Hotel (2½ miles) and Feughside Inn (1 mile), white stones at drive end; approximately 300 metres from car park for Forestry Commission's own Shooting Greens walks.
Admission £1.00 Children 50p
SUNDAY 24th APRIL 2 – 5 pm. to 15th May by arrangement. Tel: 0330 850221
40% to Welfare Fund, Roxburghe House Hospice

THE BURN HOUSE & THE BURN GARDEN HOUSE, Glenesk ♿ (no toilet facility)
(London Goodenough Trust for Overseas Graduates)
Burn House built in 1790. Grounds (190 acres) including 2½ mile river path by River North Esk. Tea in Mansion House. Route: Edzell 1 mile. Front gate situated on north side of River North Esk bridge on B966.
Admission £1.50 Children 75p
SUNDAY 29th MAY 2 – 5 pm
20% to Save the Children Fund
20% to the Army Benevolent Fund

LOCHABER, BADENOCH & STRATHSPEY
(HIGHLAND REGION)

District Organiser:	**Mrs R Philippi,** Moy Lodge, Roy Bridge, Lochaber
Hon. Treasurer:	**Mr R Philippi,** Moy Lodge, Roy Bridge, Lochaber

DATES OF OPENING

Ardtornish, Lochaline .... Daily 1 April – 31 October 10am – 6pm

Achnacarry, Spean Bridge .... Sunday 22 May	2 – 5.30pm
Ardtornish, Lochaline .... Sunday 29 May	2 – 5pm
Ard-Daraich, Ardgour .... Sunday 5 June	2 – 5pm
Aberarder, Kinlochlaggan .... Sunday 25 September	2.30 – 5.30pm
Ardverikie, Kinlochlaggan .... Sunday 25 September	2.30 – 5.30pm

ABERADER, Kinlochlaggan
(Lady Fielden)
Flower and kitchen garden. Marvellous views down Loch Laggan. Teas. To be run in conjunction with Ardverikie.
Admission £1.00
SUNDAY 25th SEPTEMBER 2.30 – 5.30 pm
40% to Kinlochlaggan Village Hall

ACHNACARRY, Spean Bridge &
(Sir Donald & Lady Cameron of Locheil)
The jewel in the crown of Lochaber's gardens, a wild profusion of rhododendrons, azaleas and flowers along the banks of the River Arkaig, in the park and around the house. Clan Cameron Museum. Forest walks. Teas in Village Hall, 200 yards from the house. Flower and produce stall. Route: Spean Bridge, left of A82, half a mile north of Spean Bridge by Commando Monument, marked Gairlochy. At Gairlochy turn right off B8005.
Admission: House & Garden £2.00 Children under 12 free.
SUNDAY 22nd MAY 2 – 5.30 pm
40% to Multiple Sclerosis Society

ARD-DARAICH, Ardgour, by Fort William
(Major David & Lady Edith Maclaren)
Seven acre hill garden, in a spectacular setting, with many fine and uncommon rhododendrons, an interesting selection of trees and shrubs and a large collection of camellias, acers and sorbus. Home made teas in house. Cake and plant stall. Route: west from Fort William, across the Corran Ferry and a mile on the right further west.
Admission £1.00 Children & OAPs 50p
SUNDAY 5th JUNE 2 – 5 pm
40% to Multiple Sclerosis Society (Fort William branch)

ARDTORNISH, Lochaline, Morvern
(Mrs John Raven)
Garden of interesting mature conifers, rhododendrons, deciduous trees and shrubs set amidst magnificent scenery. Route: A884. Lochaline 3 miles.
Admission (collection box) £1.00 Children free.
DAILY 1st APRIL to 31st OCTOBER 10 am – 6 pm
Donation to Scotland's Gardens Scheme
SUNDAY 29th MAY. Home made teas in the main house from 2 to 5 pm
40% to Morvern Parish Church

ARDVERIKIE, Kinlochlaggan &
(Ardverikie Estate Company)
Lovely setting on Loch Laggan, walled garden, herbaceous, shrubs, arboretum with forest walks. Architecturally amazing house. Teas at Aberader. On A86 between Newtonmore and Spean Bridge – entrance on left at east end of Loch Laggan, by gate lodge and over bridge. To be run in conjunction with Aberader.
Admission £1.00 Children under 12 free OAPs 50p
SUNDAY 25th SEPTEMBER 2.30 – 5.30 pm
40% to British Red Cross Society

MIDLOTHIAN
(LOTHIAN REGION)

District Organiser: **The Hon Mrs C J Dalrymple,** OBE, Oxenfoord Mains, Dalkeith EH22 2PF

Area Organisers: **Mrs George Burnet,** Rose Court, Inveresk

Mrs H Faulkner, Currie Lee, Nr Pathhead EH37 5XB

Hon. Treasurer: **Mr K Inverarity,** Royal Bank of Scotland, 63 High Street, Dalkeith EH22 1JA

DATES OF OPENING

Arniston, Gorebridge .... Tuesdays, Thursdays & Sundays
July – mid-September

Greenfield Lodge, Lasswade .... First Tuesday of each month
March-September incl. 2 – 5pm
All year, by appointment

Prestonhall, Pathhead .... Sunday 6 March	2 – 5pm
Greenfield Lodge, Lasswade .... Sunday 13 March	2 – 4.30pm
Greenfield Lodge, Lasswade .... Sunday 27 March	2 – 4.30pm
Arniston, Gorebridge.. Sunday 17 April	2 – 5.30pm
Lasswade Spring Gardens .... Sat & Sun 14/15 May	2.30 – 5.30pm
Penicuik House, Penicuik....................................... Sunday 29 May	2 – 5.30pm
Lasswade Summer Gardens .... Sat & Sun 25/26 June	2 – 5.30pm

ARNISTON, Gorebridge ♿ (partly)

(Mrs Aedrian Dundas-Bekker)

William Adam Mansion House. Daffodils in sunken garden which was laid out in the late 18th century with bridges incorporating stones from old Parliament House. Tour of House £2. Teas. Route: B6372 Gorebridge 2 miles.

Admission 50p Children 10p

TUESDAYS, THURSDAYS & SUNDAYS from JULY to MID-SEPTEMBER Groups by appointment Tel: 0875 30238

SUNDAY 17th APRIL 2 – 5.30 pm. Borthwick & District Pipe Band will play during the afternoon.

40% to the Thistle Foundation

GREENFIELD LODGE, Lasswade ♿

(Dr Alan & Mrs Helen Dickinson)

A 1½ acre wooded garden with a very wide range of flowering shrubs, unusual herbaceous plants, ornamental grasses, alpines and bulbs, including the National Chionodoxa Collection. The garden, at its peak in spring, is designed to give colour and interest throughout the year. Early 19th century bow-fronted house with later additions (not open). Teas. Plant stall. Parking. No dogs please. Off the Loanhead to Lasswade road (A768) at the end of Green Lane, off Church Road.

Admission £1.00 Careful children free.

FIRST TUESDAY OF EACH MONTH, MARCH – SEPTEMBER inclusive: 2 – 5 pm

SUNDAYS 13th & 27th MARCH 2 – 4.30 pm

Open throughout the year by appointment. Tel: 031-663 9338 the day before proposed visit.

40% to Shelter (Scotland)

LASSWADE SPRING GARDENS ♿ (some)

Gordon Bank	Small cottage garden designed for easy management.
Beechpark	Flower arranger's garden, informally laid out with interesting plants, flowering & evergreen shrubs for cutting all year round.
Wester Riggs	Recently redesigned garden with shrubs, small trees & herbaceous plants. Also an established fish pond.
Fermain	One-third of an acre with oriental touches. Rhododendrons & heathers. Natural and formal ponds.
Edenkerry	Original part is mainly shrubs and trees planted for foliage shape and colour. Added part through moon gate is wilder.

Home made teas. Plant stall. Off B704 between Lasswade & Bonnyrigg.

Admission £1.50

SATURDAY & SUNDAY 14th & 15th MAY 2.30 – 5.30 pm

40% to Multiple Sclerosis Society (Lothian branch)

LASSWADE SUMMER GARDENS &. (some)

Broomieknowe is a conservation area above the south bank of the N. Esk. Developed in the 19th century for the owners of paper mills and those seeking clean air from Edinburgh it contains gardens of great variety. Some enjoy spacious views of the valley and Pentlands, others benefit from unusual mature trees and all are sheltered by stone walls. Among the eight on view there is a heather specialist, a modern "Victorian Folly", ideas to deal with sloping ground, emphasis on minimal maintenance, small cottage and ½ acre traditional. This is a further group to those opening in Lasswade in spring 1994. Plant stalls. Home made tea at The Elms. Off B704 between Lasswade and Bonnyrigg. Admission £1.50 includes all gardens

SATURDAY & SUNDAY 25th & 26th JUNE 2 – 5.30 pm
20% to Children's Hospice Association, Scotland
20% to WRVS Midlothian

PENICUIK HOUSE, Penicuik &.

(Sir John D Clerk Bt)

House converted from 18th century stables in landscaped grounds with ornamental lakes. Plant stall. Home baked tea in house. Admission to house £2.00. On A766 road to Carlops. Penicuik two miles.
Admission £1.00 Children 50p

SUNDAY 29th MAY 2 – 5.30 pm
40% to Episcopal Church of St James-the-less, Penicuik

PRESTONHALL, Pathhead &.

(Major J H Callander)

Extensive parklands with carpets of snowdrops. Strong shoes recommended for woodland walks. Home made teas. Half a mile due east from A68 – well signposted.
Admission £1.00 Children & cars free

SUNDAY 6th MARCH 2 – 5 pm.
40% to Malcolm Sargent Cancer Fund for Children

MORAY & WEST BANFF
(GRAMPIAN REGION)

District Organiser: **Mrs A G Laing,** Relugas House, Dunphail, Forres IV36 0QL

Hon. Treasurer: **Mrs H D P Brown,** Tilliedivie House, Relugas, Dunphail, Forres IV36 0QL

DATES OF OPENING

Ballindalloch Castle	Sunday 24 April	10am – 5pm
Altyre, Forres	Sunday 15 May	2 – 6pm
Dallas Lodge, Dallas	Sunday 12 June	2 – 6pm
Gordonstoun, Duffus	Sunday 26 June	2 – 6pm
Relugas House, by Forres	Sunday 28 August	2 – 6pm

ALTYRE, Forres &

(Sir William Gordon-Cumming)
Attractive woodland and water setting with colourful shrubs, lawns, etc. All dogs on lead please. 2 miles south of Forres on A940 Forres/Grantown road. Teas.
Admission £1.50 Children 50p
SUNDAY 15th MAY 2 – 6 pm
40% to Moray Scanner Appeal

BALLINDALLOCH CASTLE, Ballindalloch &

(Mr & Mrs Oliver Russell)
Lovely situation by River Spey. Daffodils, rock garden. Castle open to public 10 am – 5 pm. Tea room. Shop. Audio-visual.
Admission £3.75 Children free
SUNDAY 24th APRIL 10 am – 5 pm
40% to Cancer Relief Macmillan Fund

DALLAS LODGE, Dallas, by Forres & (partly)

(David Houldsworth, Esq)
Lawns and borders, azaleas and rhododendrons with many varieties of daffodils in natural woodland setting around loch. Tea in Houldsworth Institute, Dallas village. 6 miles from Forres on B9010.
Admission £1.50 Children 50p
SUNDAY 12th JUNE 2 – 6 pm
40% to Cancer Relief Macmillan Fund

GORDONSTOUN, Duffus, near Elgin &

(The Headmaster, Gordonstoun School)
School grounds; Gordonstoun House (Georgian House of 1775/6 incorporating earlier 17th century house built for 1st Marquis of Huntly) and School Chapel – both open. Unique circle of former farm buildings known as the Round Square. Teas. Duffus village 4 miles from Elgin on B9012.
Admission £1.50 Children 50p
SUNDAY 26th JUNE 2 – 6 pm
All takings to Scotland's Gardens Scheme

RELUGAS HOUSE, by Forres & (partly)

(Mrs A G Laing)
Varied garden in beautiful setting by River Divie. Rock garden. Woodland walks up the Doune of Relugas. Teas. Entrance opposite Randolph's Leap on B9007. Forres 7 miles. Carrbridge 15 miles.
Admission £1.50 Children 50p
SUNDAY 28th AUGUST 2 – 6 pm

PERTH & KINROSS
(TAYSIDE REGION)

Joint District Organisers:	**Mrs M E Hamilton,** Glencarse House, Glencarse
	Mrs Charles Moncrieff, Easter Elcho, Rhynd PH2 8QQ
Area Organisers:	**Mrs D J W Anstice,** Broomhill, Abernethy PH2 9LQ
	Mrs A H Campbell, 24 Langside Drive, Comrie
	Mrs C Dunphie, Wester Cloquhat, Bridge of Cally PH10 7JP
	Mrs A Leslie, Seasyde House, Errol PH2 7TA
	Mrs Colin Maitland Dougall, Dowhill, Kelty, Fife KY4 0HZ
	Mrs Athol Price, Urlar Farm, Aberfeldy PH15 2EW
Hon. Treasurer:	**Major R N Jardine Paterson,** Balquharrie, Muthill PH5 2BP

DATES OF OPENING

Auchleeks, Calvine	Wednesdays 22 June – 3 August	2 – 5pm
Bolfracks, Aberfeldy	Daily 1 April – 31 October	10am – 6pm
Cluny House, Aberfeldy	Daily 1 March – 31 October	10am – 6pm
Dowhill, Cleish	Thursdays in May and June	1.30 – 4pm
Lude, Blair Atholl	Thursdays 16 June – 11 August, excl. 30 June	11am – 5pm
Scone Palace, Perth	1 April – 10 October: weekdays	9.30am – 5pm
	Sundays	1.30 – 5pm
	July & August:	10am – 5pm

Glendoick, by Perth	Sunday 1 May	2 – 5pm
Branklyn, Perth	Sunday 8 May	9.30am-sunset
Glendoick, by Perth	Sunday 8 May	2 – 5pm
Glendoick, by Perth	Sunday 15 May	2 – 5pm
Stobhall, by Perth	Sunday 15 May	2 – 6pm
Easter Dunbarnie, Bridge of Earn	Sat & Sun 21/22 May	2 – 6pm
Ardvorlich, Lochearnhead	Sunday 22 May	2 – 6pm
Glendoick, by Perth	Sunday 22 May	2 – 5pm
Kennacoil House, Dunkeld	Sunday 22 May	2 – 6pm
Wester Dalqueich, Carnbo	Wednesday 25 May	2 – 5pm
Battleby, Redgorton	Sunday 5 June	2 – 5pm
Murthly Castle, by Dunkeld	Sunday 5 June	2 – 6pm
Rossie Priory, Inchture	Sunday 5 June	2 – 6pm
Branklyn, Perth	Sunday 12 June	9.30am-sunset
Cloquhat Gardens, Bridge of Cally	Sunday 12 June	2 – 6pm
The Bank House, Glenfarg	Sunday 12 June	2 – 6pm
Wester Dalqueich, Carnbo	Wednesday 6 July	2 – 5pm
Dunbarney House, Bridge of Earn	Sunday 10 July	2 – 6pm
Boreland, Killin	Sunday 24 July	2 – 5.30pm
Wester Dalqueich, Carnbo	Wednesday 3 August	2 – 5pm
Cluniemore, Pitlochry	Sunday 7 August	2 – 5.30pm
Drummond Castle Gardens, Muthill	Sunday 7 August	2 – 6pm
Megginch Castle, Errol	Sunday 14 August	2 – 5pm

ARDVORLICH, Lochearnhead
(Mr & Mrs Sandy Stewart)
Beautiful glen with rhododendrons (species and modern hybrids) grown in wild conditions amid oaks and birches. Gum boots advisable. Teas. On south Lochearn road 3 miles from Lochearnhead, 4½ miles from St Fillans.
Admision £1.00 Children under 12 free
SUNDAY 22nd MAY 2 – 6 pm
40% to St Columba's Hospice

AUCHLEEKS HOUSE, Calvine, Pitlochry
(Rear Admiral & Mrs John Mackenzie)
Lovely old fashioned walled garden with large herbaceous borders in scenic setting. Rock garden. No dogs please. Home made teas. Calvine 4½ miles. Trinafour ½ mile. Take B847 Kinloch Rannoch road from Calvine.
Admission £1.50 Children under 12 free
WEDNESDAYS 22nd JUNE – 3rd AUGUST inclusive, 2 – 5 pm
40% to Toberargan Surgery Equipment Fund, Pitlochry

BATTLEBY, Redgorton, Perth   ♿
(Scottish Natural Heritage)
15 acres around Battleby House and Centre. Rhododendrons, azaleas, specimen trees, woodland walks, outdoor display centre, indoor auditorium/video programme. Plant stall. Tea in Centre. One mile from main A9, 5 miles north of Perth, via B8063.
Admission £1.50. Accompanied children under 14 free. OAPs 50p
SUNDAY 5th JUNE 2 – 5 pm
40% to Scottish Wildlife Trust (Perthshire branch)

BOLFRACKS, Aberfeldy
(Mr J D Hutchison, CBE)
Garden overlooking the Tay valley. Walled garden with borders of trees, shrubs and perennials. Burn garden with rhododendrons, azaleas, primulas, meconopsis, etc., in woodland setting. Masses of bulbs in spring. Good autumn colour. No dogs please. Limited range of plants for sale. Route: 2 miles west of Aberfeldy on A827. White gates and Lodge on left of road. Not suitable for wheelchairs.
Admission £1.50 Children under 12 free
DAILY 1st APRIL to 31st OCTOBER 10 am – 6 pm
Donation to Scotland's Gardens Scheme

BORELAND, Killin   ♿
(Mrs Angus Stroyan)
A varied garden but with border the main feature. Very pretty walk along river leading to arboretum. Teas. Plant stall. Route: through Killin, first turning left over bridge after Bridge of Lochay Hotel. House approximately 2 miles on left.
Admission £1.50 Children over 12 50p
SUNDAY 24th JULY 2 – 5.30 pm
40% to Cancer Research

BRANKLYN, Perth
(The National Trust for Scotland)
Rhododendrons, alpines, herbaceous and peat garden plants from all over the world.
Cars free. Tea and coffee. On A85 Perth/Dundee road.
Admission £2.00 Children & OAPs £1.00
SUNDAY 8th MAY and SUNDAY 12th JUNE 9.30 am – sunset
40% to NTS Threave Bursary Fund
For other opening details see page 130

CLOQUHAT GARDENS, Bridge of Cally ♿ (partly)
CLOQUHAT. (Colonel Peter Dunphie CBE)
Fine views down to river. Azaleas, rhododendrons, shrubs. Woodland and burnside
gardens. Terrace with rock plants. Walled garden.
WESTER CLOQUHAT. (Brigadier & Mrs Christopher Dunphie)
Small garden started in 1989. Splendid situation. Several mixed borders with wide
variety of shrubs and herbaceous plants. Heather bank. Teas and plant stall. No dogs
please. Turn off A93 just north of Bridge of Cally and follow yellow signs one mile.
Admission to both gardens £1.50 Children 50p
SUNDAY 12th JUNE 2 – 6 pm
40% to S.S.A.F.A.

CLUNIEMORE, Pitlochry ♿
(Sir David & Lady Butter)
Water garden, rock garden. Woodlands in beautiful setting. Shrubs, herbaceous borders,
annual border and roses. Plant stall. Tea, biscuits and ice cream. Parties by appointment
any time. On A9 Pitlochry bypass.
Admission £2.00 Children over 12 50p
SUNDAY 7th AUGUST 2 – 5.30 pm
40% to Duke of Edinburgh's Award Scheme

CLUNY HOUSE, Aberfeldy
(Mr J & Mrs W Mattingley)
Woodland garden with many specimen trees, shrubs and rhododendrons, with extensive
views of Strathtay to Ben Lawers. An outstanding collection of primulas, meconopsis,
nomocharis, cardiocrinums and other Himalayan plants. Autumn colour. Plant stall. No
dogs please. 3½ miles from Aberfeldy on Weem to Strathtay road.
Admission £1.50 Children under 16 free
DAILY 1st MARCH to 31st OCTOBER 10 am – 6 pm
Donation to Scotland's Gardens Scheme

DOWHILL, Cleish
(Mr & Mrs Colin Maitland Dougall)
A garden started six years ago to complement the magnificent, mature trees. Ponds and
water garden. Woodland walks to ruins of Dowhill Castle. Small plant stall. Entrance
three-quarters of a mile from Exit 5 off M90, on B9097 Crook of Devon road.
Admission £1.00
THURSDAYS during MAY and JUNE 1.30 – 4 pm
40% to Arthritis Council for Research

DRUMMOND CASTLE GARDENS, Muthill ♿
(Grimsthorpe & Drummond Castle Trust Ltd.)
The gardens of Drummond Castle were originally laid out in 1630 by John Drummond, 2nd Earl of Perth. In 1830 the parterre was changed to an Italian style. One of the most interesting features is the multi-faceted sundial designed by John Mylne, Master Mason to Charles I. The formal garden is said to be one of the finest in Europe and is the largest of its type in Scotland. Open daily 2 – 6 pm (last entrance 5 pm). Entrance 2 miles south of Crieff on Muthill road (A822).
Admission £2.00 Children & OAPs £1.00
SUNDAY 7th AUGUST 2 – 6 pm. Teas, raffle, entertainments & stalls.
40% to British Limbless Ex-Servicemen's Association

DUNBARNEY HOUSE, Bridge of Earn ♿
(Mr & Mrs Robert C M Rankin)
Walled garden attached to house, with much new planting. Formal lawns, roses and shrubs leading to orchard encompassing new rose tunnels. Beech woodland walk. Specimen trees in extensive grounds. Teas. Plant stall. 5 minutes from M90, exit 9. Take B935 out of Bridge of Earn (Forgandenny road) Buses from Perth stop at gates.
Admission £1.50 Children free
SUNDAY 10th JULY 2 – 6 pm
40% to National Autistic Society

EASTER DUNBARNIE, Bridge of Earn ♿
(The Hon Ranald & Mrs Noel Paton)
Fine trees and shrubs, rhododendrons, azaleas, meconopsis and primulas. Woodland walks. No dogs. Teas. Plant and produce stalls. 5 minutes from M90, exit 9. Take B935 out of Bridge of Earn (Forgandenny road).
Admission £2.00 Children 50p
SATURDAY 21st MAY (garden only) 2 – 6 pm
SUNDAY 22nd MAY 2 – 6 pm
40% to National Art Collections Fund

GLENDOICK, Perth ♿ (partly)
(Mr & Mrs Peter Cox & family)
Classic Georgian house about 1746 (not open). Garden full of interesting plants and trees, with extended area of meandering paths to explore in the famous rhododendron woodland. Nursery also open. No dogs please. Acorn Restaurant nearby. Garden centre open 9 am – 6 pm. On A85 Perth/Dundee road. Glencarse 2 miles, Perth 8 miles, Dundee 11 miles.
Admission £1.50 Children under 5 free
SUNDAYS 1st, 8th, 15th, 22nd MAY 2 – 5 pm
40% to World Wide Fund for Nature

KENNACOIL HOUSE, Dunkeld
(Mrs Walter Steuart Fothringham)
Informal to wild garden with herbaceous border, shrubs, rhododendrons and azaleas on hillside with exceptional view. Burn with water garden. Teas. Plant stall. No dogs please. Dunkeld 3 miles, off Crieff road A822.
Admission £1.50 Children under 12 50p
SUNDAY 22nd MAY 2 – 6 pm
40% to Scottish Society for the Mentally Handicapped

EDENKERRY, BROOMIEKNOWE, LASSWADE
(Mr and Mrs Colin Thompson)

Lasswade Gardens, Saturday and Sunday, 14th/15th May, 2.30-5.30 p.m.

CORTACHY CASTLE, KIRRIEMUIR
(The Earl and Countess of Airlie)

Sunday, 29th May, 2-6 p.m.

SHEPHERD HOUSE, INVERESK
(Sir Charles and Lady Fraser)

Thursday, 5th May – Sunday, 8th May; Thursday, 9th June; 2-5.30 p.m.
and with Inveresk Village Opening, Sunday, 10th July

BAITLAWS, LAMINGTON, BIGGAR
(Mr and Mrs M. Maxwell Stuart)

Sunday, 31st July, 2-6 p.m.

LUDE, Blair Atholl ♿
(Mr & Mrs W G Gordon)
Fine trees, roses, peonies, shrubs and herbaceous plants, fruit and vegetables in "secret" walled garden. Blair Atholl 1¼ miles, entrance is opposite Tilt Hotel.
Admission £1.50 Children under 16 free
THURSDAYS 16th & 23rd JUNE, all THURSDAYS in JULY and 4th & 11th AUGUST 11am – 5pm
Donation to Scotland's Gardens Scheme

MEGGINCH CASTLE, Errol ♿
(Captain Drummond of Megginch & Baroness Strange)
15th century turreted castle (not open) with Gothic courtyard and pagoda dovecote. 1,000 year old yews and topiary work in natural surroundings. Colourful annual border in walled garden. Astrological garden. On A85 between Perth (9½miles) and Dundee (12 miles). Look for Lodge on south side of road.
Admission £1.50 Children free
SUNDAY 14th AUGUST 2 – 5 pm
40% to All Saints Church, Glencarse

MURTHLY CASTLE, by Dunkeld ♿
(Mr R Steuart Fothringham)
Early 14th century Royal hunting lodge with 15th century tower and 17th, 18th and 19th century additions. Extensive well-wooded policies on River Tay, with long avenues of magnificent trees. Sunken terrace with rhododendrons and azaleas. Formal walled garden. Private chapel in grounds. Air rifle range. Pipe band. Tea. Birnam 2 miles from west gate. Turn off A9 two miles south of Birnam approaching from north only. Murthly is three-quarters mile from east gate. B9099 Stanley/Caputh road.
Admission including chapel £1.50 Children 50p
SUNDAY 5th JUNE 2 – 6 pm
20% to Guide Dogs for the Blind
20% to St Columba's Hospice

ROSSIE PRIORY, Inchture ♿
(Mr G R Spencer)
Arboretum with marked specimen trees, woodland walks, water gardens and herbaceous borders. Extensive lawns with lovely views over the Tay to Fife. Home baked teas. Produce stall and raffle. Entrance east of Inchture on A85. Dundee 8 miles. Perth 13 miles.
Admission £1.50 Children 5 – 15 75p
SUNDAY 5th JUNE 2 – 6 pm
40% to Marie Curie Cancer Care

SCONE PALACE, Perth ♿
(The Earl of Mansfield)
Extensive and well laid out grounds and a magnificent pinetum dating from 1848; there is a Douglas Fir raised from the original seed sent from America in 1824. The Woodland Garden has attractive walks amongst the rhododendrons and azaleas and leads into the Monks' Playgreen and Friar's Den of the former Abbey of Scone. The Palace of Scone lies adjacent to the Moot Hill where the Kings of Scots were crowned. Full catering by the Palace staff. Adventure playground. Special rates for season tickets and parties. Route A93. Perth 2 miles.
Admission Palace & Grounds £4.20 Children £2.30 OAPs £3.40
FRIDAY 1st APRIL to MONDAY 10th OCTOBER. Weekdays 9.30 am – 5 pm, Sundays 1.30 – 5 pm. JULY and AUGUST 10 am – 5 pm.
Donation to Scotland's Gardens Scheme

STOBHALL, by Perth ♿
(The Earl & Countess of Perth)
Group of early and medieval buildings, including castle and chapel with painted ceiling on ridge high above River Tay. Site of dwelling houses since 14th century, associated with two queens of Scotland. Early topiary garden, also wild garden and walk in woodland glen. Terrace walk below castle. Refreshments. 1½ miles north of Guildtown on A93 midway Perth/Blairgowrie.
Admission to gardens & chapel £2 Children £1.00
SUNDAY 15th MAY 2 – 6 pm
40% to Innerpeffray Library

THE BANK HOUSE, Glenfarg ♿ (mostly)
(Mr & Mrs C B Lascelles)
A large garden (for the centre of a village) in two parts. Behind the house a tunnel of apple trees leads from a stone-paved area into the main garden of shrubs and herbaceous plants, many of them unusual. Pond, fountains, sculpture; raised-bed vegetable system, organic methods throughout; advanced compost-making equipment. Across the road, water cascades down steps to a further garden with a large Yin-Yang bed, from where a bridge crosses the stream to a field in which a wildlife pond has been created and ornamental trees planted. Gardening's ultimate challenge – a wildflower meadow – is being attempted at the furthest end. Teas at nearby hotel. Interesting plant stall. Situated 50 yards down side road by Glenfarg Hotel.
Admission £1.50 Children & OAPs 75p
SUNDAY 12th JUNE 2 – 6 pm
40% to Glenfarg Village Hall

WESTER DALQUEICH, Carnbo ♿ (partly)
(Mr & Mrs D S Roulston)
Two acre garden by the Ochil Hills, 600ft above sea level. Interesting herbaceous and rock plants, shrubs with informal planting in the glades. Teas. Plant stall. Carnbo village is west of Milnathort. Leave A91 near Carnbo village and travel north for ½ mile.
Admission £1.00 Children & OAPs 50p
WEDNESDAYS 25th MAY, 6th JULY & 3rd AUGUST 2 – 5 pm
40% to Strathcarron Hospice, Denny

RENFREW, INVERCLYDE & EASTWOOD
(STRATHCLYDE REGION)

Joint District Organisers: **Mrs J R Hutton,** Auchenclava, Finlaystone,
                                      Langbank PA14 6TJ

                                      Mrs Daphne Ogg, Nittingshill, Kilmacolm PA13 4SG

Area Organisers: **Lady Denholm,** Newton of Bell Trees, Lochwinnoch PA12 4JL

                                      Mr Jim May, Greenbank Garden, Clarkston,
                                      Glasgow G76 8RD

Hon. Treasurer: **Mrs Jean Gillan,** 28 Walkerston Avenue, Largs KA30 8ER

DATES OF OPENING

Church Street, Kilbarchan	17 April – 4 September (excl.July) Tuesdays, Thursdays, most weekends, by appointment	
Knapps, Kilmacolm	March – September, weekdays, by appointment	
Ardgowan, Inverkip	Sunday 20 February	2 – 5pm
Finlaystone, Langbank	Sunday 10 April	2 – 5pm
Calderbank & Calderbank Cottage, Lochwinnoch	Sunday 15 May	2 – 5pm
Renfrew Central Nursery	Sat & Sun 21/22 May	1 – 5pm
Formakin Estate, by Bishopton	Monday 30 May	11am – 5pm
Duchal, Kilmacolm	Sunday 19 June	2 – 5pm
Lunderston, Ardgowan	Sunday 26 June	2 – 5pm
Greenbank Garden, Clarkston	Sunday 31 July	2 – 5pm

ARDGOWAN, Inverkip ♿ (not advisable if wet)
(Sir Houston and Lady Shaw-Stewart)
Woodland walks carpeted with snowdrops. (Strong footwear advised). Tea in house. Snowdrop stall, souvenirs, home produce. Inverkip 1½ miles. Glasgow/Largs buses in Inverkip.
Admission £1.00 Children under 10 free
SUNDAY 20th FEBRUARY 2 – 5 pm
40% to The Erskine Hospital

CALDERBANK & CALDERBANK COTTAGE, Lochwinnoch
(Sheriff Principal & Mrs Norman MacLeod, Mr & Mrs J Gillespie)
Bluebell hill. Riverside and woodland walks. Duck pond. Rhododendrons, azaleas, young and mature trees. Strong shoes advised, dogs on leads and take us as you find us. Plant stall. Tea. One mile from Lochwinnoch off A760 on B786.
Admission £1.50 Children over 10 50p
SUNDAY 15th MAY 2 – 5 pm
20% to Dyslexia Scotwest
20% to St Vincent's Hospice, Howwood

CHURCH STREET, Kilbarchan
(Mr & Mrs Caldwell)
This secluded garden in the heart of Old Kilbarchan is full of charm and interest. Great variety packed into a small space, bordered by a burn. Close to The Weaver's Cottage, National Trust for Scotland.
17th APRIL to 4th SEPTEMBER, excluding JULY.
Tuesdays & Thursdays & most weekends, by appointment Tel. 05057 03282
40% to Cancer Relief Macmillan Fund

DUCHAL, Kilmacolm ♿
(The Lord and Lady Maclay)
18th century walled garden, clipped hollies, azaleas. Old fashioned roses, shrubs and herbaceous borders with fruit orchards and vegetable garden. Loch and woodlands. Lily pond. Plant and produce stall. Teas under cover. Kilmacolm 1 mile, B786. Greenock/Glasgow bus via Bridge of Weir; Knapps Loch stop is ¼ mile from garden.
Admission £1.00 Children & OAPs 60p
SUNDAY 19th JUNE 2 – 5 pm
40% to Strathcarron Hospice, Denny

FINLAYSTONE, Langbank ♿
(Mr & Mrs George G MacMillan)
Historic connection with John Knox and Robert Burns. Richly varied gardens with unusual plants overlooking the Clyde. Profusion of daffodils and early rhododendrons. Waterfalls & pond. Woodland walks with play and picnic areas, fort and "Eye-opener" Centre. Ranger service. Home baking stall. Plant stall. Teas in Celtic Tree. Admission to House: £1.40. Children & OAPs 80p. Langbank station 1 mile. On A8 west of Langbank, 10 minutes by car west of Glasgow Airport.
Admission £1.50 Children & OAPs £1.00
SUNDAY 10th APRIL 2 – 5 pm
20% to Quarrier's Village
20% to Erskine Hospital

FORMAKIN ESTATE, by Bishopton ♿ (partly)
(The Formakin Trust)
Mansion house (internally unfinished), gatehouses, stables, courtyard, tower house and meal mill in landscaped grounds. Woodland and formal gardens designed 1903 – 1913 by Sir Robert Lorimer. Fountain Gardens have now been restored as well as the complete restoration works to Mill Lade, the lake, top pond, burns and the Plum walkway. The estate also has meeting rooms, children's adventure playground, visitor centre, exhibition area, and Courtyard Tea Room. Admission to House: 50p. Bishopton 1½ miles. Bus route: Bishopton village. (No Season Tickets to be used on this day)
Admission £1.50 Children £1.00 Family £4.00
MONDAY 30th MAY 11 am – 5 pm
40% to Formakin Trust

GREENBANK GARDEN, Clarkston, Glasgow ♿
(The National Trust for Scotland)
Walled demonstration gardens. Woodland garden trail. Scottish Croquet Association Open Day. Plant stall. Tea room open 2 – 5 pm. Clarkston 1 mile. Bus: Clydeside no.2, Strathclyde no.66C to Mearnskirk or Newton Mearns.
Admission £2.00 Children & OAPs £1.00
SUNDAY 31st JULY 9.30 am – sunset. Charity opening 2 – 5 pm.
40% to NTS Threave Bursary Fund
For other opening details see page 141

KNAPPS, Houston Road, Kilmacolm
(Dr & Mr Morris)
A 10 acre garden overlooking Knapps Loch comprising woodland, bog, informal paths and herbaceous borders. Well planted, hedged and landscaped in the Twenties but later overgrown, the gardens are now being reclaimed and restored with many new trees, shrubs, rhododendrons, bulbs, alpines, etc., planted amongst many older and well established specimens. Interesting plants raised from seed may be available for sale. Take first road right entering village from Bridge of Weir.
Admission £2.00 Children 50p OAPs £1.00
MARCH to SEPTEMBER, Weekdays by appointment: 0505 87 2774 daytime.
40% to Scottish Society for the Mentally Handicapped

LUNDERSTON, Ardgowan, Inverkip ♿
(Mr J L Kinloch)
Landscaped garden with fine views across the Firth of Clyde. Wide selection of plants including rhododendron bank, heather garden, roses, herbaceous and well laid out vegetable garden. Plant stall. Teas. Enter Ardgowan at North Lodge and follow signs.
Admission £1.00 Children over 10 & OAPs 50p
SUNDAY 26th JUNE 2 – 5 pm
20% to Ardgowan Hospice and 20% to Erskine Hospital

RENFREW CENTRAL NURSERY, Hawkhead Road, Paisley ♿
(Renfrew District Council)
Three-quarters of an acre under glass, intensively cropped, associated with Open Day demonstrations. Exhibitions of related crafts, countryside interpretation, etc. Entertainments, etc. Tea served in marquee. Plant stall.
Admission £1.00 Children & OAPs 50p
SATURDAY and SUNDAY 21st and 22nd MAY 1 – 5 pm
40% to Erskine Hospital

ROSS, CROMARTY, SKYE & INVERNESS
(HIGHLAND REGION)

District Organiser: **Lady Lister-Kaye,** Aigas House, Beauly IV4 7AD

Area Organisers: **Mrs Robin Fremantle,** Scatwell, Muir of Ord IV6 7QG

Hon. Treasurer: **Mr Kenneth Haselock,** 2 Tomich, Strathglass, By Beauly IV4 7LZ

DATES OF OPENING

Abriachan Garden Nursery	Daily all year	9am – dusk
Aigas House & Field Centre	1 May – 30 September	
Brin School Fields, Flichity	Daily June – September	8.30am – 7pm
	Sundays	2 – 5pm
Dunvegan Castle, Isle of Skye	21 March – 29 October	10am – 5pm
Glamaig, Braes, Isle of Skye	Daily Easter – mid-September	
Leckmelm Shrubbery & Arboretum	Daily 1 April – 30 September	10am – 6pm
Sea View, Dundonnell	Daily Easter – mid-October	10am-dusk
Inverewe, Poolewe	Saturday 30 April	9.30am-sunset
Allangrange, Munlochy	Sunday 8 May	2 – 5.30pm
Lochalsh Woodland Garden, Balmacara	Saturday 14 May	1 – 5.30pm
Laggan House, Scaniport	Sunday 22 May	2 – 5pm
Attadale, Strathcarron	Saturday 28 May	2 – 6pm
House of Gruinard, by Laide	Saturday 28 May	2 – 6pm
Aldourie Castle, Inverness	Sunday 29 May	2 – 5pm
Novar, Evanton	Sunday 29 May	2 – 6pm
Tournaig, Poolewe	Wednesday 1 June	2 – 6pm
Inveran Lodge, Poolewe	Saturday 4 June	2 – 6pm
Brahan, Dingwall	Sunday 5 June	2 – 5.30pm
Kyllachy, Tomatin	Sunday 5 June	2 – 5.30pm
Dundonnell, by Little Loch Broom	Thursday 9 June	2 – 5.30pm
Achnashellach Station House	Fri & Sat 10/11 June	10am – 6pm
Allangrange, Munlochy	Sunday 12 June	2 – 5.30pm
Dundonnell, by Little Loch Broom	Wednesday 15 June	2 – 5.30pm
Kinkell Castle, Conon Bridge	Sunday 19 June	2 – 6pm
Dundonnell, by Little Loch Broom	Thursday 7 July	2 – 5.30pm
Allangrange, Munlochy	Sunday 10 July	2 – 5.30pm
Dundonnell, by Little Loch Broom	Wednesday 13 July	2 – 5.30pm
House of Gruinard, by Laide	Wednesday 20 July	2 – 6pm
Lochalsh Woodland Garden, Balmacara	Saturday 23 July	1 – 5.30pm
Inverewe, Poolewe	Sunday 31 July	9.30am-sunset
Tournaig, Poolewe	Wednesday 3 August	2 – 6pm
Scatwell, Marybank	Sunday 7 August	2 – 6pm

ABRIACHAN GARDEN NURSERY, Loch Ness Side
(Mr & Mrs Davidson)
Primulas, hardy geraniums. Rare and unusual plants. Woodland walk and views over Loch Ness.
Admission by collection box
OPEN DAILY 9 am – dusk

ACHNASHELLACH STATION HOUSE
(Mr & Mrs P H Hainsworth)
A one acre garden started in 1975 by a plant enthusiast. Part old railway siding, part winding paths through a wild garden with a very wide range of plants and habitats. Fine mountain scenery and forest walks nearby. 9 miles east of Lochcarron. Cars take forest road (1 mile, courtesy Forestry Commission) 300 yards EAST of railway bridge over A890. Or walk 400 yards from telephone box half mile WEST of railway bridge.
Admission £1.00
FRIDAY and SATURDAY 10th and 11th JUNE 10 am – 6 pm
40% to the Association for the Protection of Rural Scotland

AIGAS HOUSE AND FIELD CENTRE, by Beauly, Inverness
(Sir John and Lady Lister-Kaye)
Aigas has a woodland walk overlooking the Beauly River with a collection of named Victorian specimen trees now being restored and extended with a garden of rockeries, herbaceous borders and shrubberies. The house is open to the public for the Field Centre shop and teas and coffees – home baking a speciality. There is also a 1½ mile nature trail and rainbow trout fishing on Aigas Loch. Route: 4½ miles from Beauly on A831 Cannich/Glen Affric road.
Admission from £1.50
MAY to SEPTEMBER
Donation to Scotland's Gardens Scheme

ALDOURIE CASTLE, Inverness
(Lt Col Angus Cameron)
Wild garden, rhododendrons and woodlands. Plant stall. Teas. Inverness 7 miles B862.
Admission £1.00
SUNDAY 29th MAY 2 – 5pm
40% to British Red Cross Society (Inverness-shire branch)

ALLANGRANGE, Munlochy, Black Isle
(Major Allan Cameron)
A formal and a wild garden containing flowering shrubs, trees and plants, especially rhododendrons, shrub roses and primulas. Plants for sale. Exhibition of botanical paintings by Elizabeth Cameron. Teas in house. Inverness 5 miles. Signposted off A9.
Admission £1.00
SUNDAYS 8th MAY, 12th JUNE and 10th JULY 2 – 5.30 pm
40% to Highland Hospice

ATTADALE, Strathcarron
(Mr & Mrs Ewen Macpherson)
Five acres of old rhododendrons, azaleas and unusual shrubs in woodland setting with views of Skye and the sea. Water gardens, with walk and sunken formal garden. Plant stall. Tea in the house. On A890 opposite village of Lochcarron.
Admission £1.50 Children & OAPs 75p
SATURDAY 28th MAY 2 – 6 pm. Other days by appointment Tel: 05202 217
40% to British Red Cross Society

BRAHAN, Dingwall
(Mr & Mrs A Matheson)
Wild garden, dell with azaleas and rhododendrons. Arboretum with labelled trees and river walk. Home made teas in house. Maryburgh 1½ miles. Take road west from Maryburgh roundabout.
Admission £1.00
SUNDAY 5th JUNE 2 – 5.30 pm
40% to Highland Hospice

 # BRIN SCHOOL FIELDS, Flichity, by Farr &
(Mr & Mrs Angus Mackenzie)
Specialist herb garden and nursery situated 700ft. above sea level beneath the dramatic backdrop of Brin Rock. Leaflet & "Walkman" tape guides available for donation. Garden divided into many smaller gardens, including edible flowers garden, children's herb garden, knot garden, cottage garden, wildflower gardens, Mediterranean conservatory, etc. Over 175 varieties of herb and wild flower plants available. The Victorian Schoolroom Shop sells herb-related books, gifts, crafts, teas and light lunches. (Lunch bookings recommended, tel: 08083 288). Inverness 15 miles, Farr 4½ miles. 7 miles from A9 junction at Daviot. On B851 Daviot/Fort Augustus road.
Admission by donation
OPEN DAILY JUNE – SEPTEMBER 8.30 am – 7 pm. Sundays 2 – 5 pm.
Donation to Scotland's Gardens Scheme

DUNDONNELL, by Little Loch Broom &
(Mr Alan and Mr Neil Roger)
Dundonnell is on Little Loch Broom 31 miles west of Garve. Garden includes a collection of bonsai. Tea. Plants for sale. Ullapool 24 miles.
Admission £1.50 Children 50p
THURSDAY 9th JUNE, WEDNESDAY 15th JUNE, THURSDAY 7th JULY, WEDNESDAY 13th JULY 2 – 5.30 pm
40% to the Army Benevolent Fund and the Police Dependants' Fund

DUNVEGAN CASTLE, Isle of Skye
(John MacLeod of MacLeod)
Dating from the 13th century and continuously inhabited by the Chiefs of MacLeod, this romantic fortress stronghold occupies a magnificent lochside setting. The gardens, originally laid out in the 18th century, have been extensively replanted and include lochside walks, woodlands and water gardens. Licensed restaurant. Two craft shops. Clan exhibition. Seal colony. Loch boat trips. Admission to Castle and Garden inclusive £4.00, students, OAPs & parties £3.60, children £2.20. Dunvegan village 1 mile, 23 miles west of Portree.
Admission to gardens £2.40 Children £1.50
MONDAY 21st MARCH – SATURDAY 29th OCTOBER 10 am – 5.30 pm (Last entry 5 pm) SUNDAYS – Gardens, craft shop and restaurant open all day. Castle 1 – 5.30 pm (Last entry 5 pm)
Donation to Scotland's Gardens Scheme

GLAMAIG, Braes, Portree, Isle of Skye
(Mr & Mrs R Townsend)
Two acres of mixed wild and informal garden with burn, waterfalls and extensive views of sea and mountains. Large collection of unusual shrubs, rhododendrons, hydrangeas, olearias, etc. Primulas, herbaceous and rock garden. Some plants for sale. 7 miles from Portree at end of B883.
Admission by collection box
OPEN DAILY EASTER TO MID-SEPTEMBER
Donation to Scotland's Gardens Scheme

HOUSE OF GRUINARD, by Laide
(The Hon Mrs Angus Maclay)
Wonderful west coast views. Herbaceous and shrub borders and water garden. Large variety of plants for sale.
Admission £1.50 Children under 16 free
SATURDAY 28th MAY and WEDNESDAY 20th JULY 2 – 6 pm
40% to Highland Hospice

INVERAN LODGE, Poolewe
(Mrs E Macdonald-Buchanan)
Interesting garden in beautiful four acre setting. Rhododendrons and some rare shrubs. Home made teas. Poolewe 1½ miles, off A832.
Admission £1.50 Children & OAPs 50p
SATURDAY 4th JUNE 2 – 6 pm
40% to Highland Hospice

INVEREWE, Poolewe &
(The National Trust for Scotland)
Garden started in 1862 by Osgood Mackenzie. Eucalyptus, rhododendrons, azaleas and many Chilean and South African plants. Himalayan lilies and many other rare plants. Visitor centre, shop and self-service restaurant.
Admission £3.00 Children & OAPs £1.50
SATURDAY 30th APRIL & SUNDAY 31st JULY 9.30 am- sunset
40% to NTS Threave Bursary Fund
For other opening details see Page 136

KINKELL CASTLE, Conon Bridge
(Mr & Mrs Gerald Ogilvie-Laing)
Sixteenth century tower house (not open). Recent plantings. Water gardens with fountains and sculpture. Teas. Plants. A835 Maryburgh/Tore road.
Admission £2.00
SUNDAY 19th JUNE 2 – 6 pm
40% to Highland Hospice

KYLLACHY, Tomatin &
(The Rt Hon The Lord & Lady Macpherson)
Rhododendrons (mainly white), azaleas, primulas, delphiniums, heather beds, herbaceous, alpines, iris, meconopsis. Water garden with stream and ponds. Walled vegetable garden. Plant stall. Tea. No dogs please. Cars free. A9 to Tomatin, turn off to Findhorn Bridge, turn west to Coignafearn. Kyllachy House one mile on right.
Admission £1.50
SUNDAY 5th JUNE 2 – 5.30 pm
40% to the Multiple Sclerosis Society in Scotland Holiday Centre

LAGGAN HOUSE, Scaniport
(Mr & Mrs Anthony Haig)
Rhododendrons, azaleas, flowering shrubs and heathers, woodland walks. Tea. Plant stall. Inverness 4 miles, on B862 Dores road.
Admission £1.50
SUNDAY 22nd MAY 2 – 5 pm
20% to the Highland Hospice
20% to the Coastal Walk for Shelter

LECKMELM SHRUBBERY & ARBORETUM, by Ullapool
(Mr & Mrs Peter Troughton)
Situated by the shore of Loch Broom 3 miles south of Ullapool on the A835 Inverness/Ullapool road. The arboretum, planted in the 1870s, fell into neglect until 1985 when the restoration to its former glory began. Specie trees, rhododendrons, azaleas and shrubs. Parking in walled garden.
Admission £1.00 Children & OAPs 50p
OPEN DAILY 1st APRIL to 30th SEPTEMBER 10 am – 6 pm
All takings to Scotland's Gardens Scheme

LOCHALSH WOODLAND GARDEN, Balmacara
(The National Trust for Scotland)
Passed to the Trust in 1953; main rhododendron planting by Ewen Cox in early '60s. A garden in the making with developing collections of rhododendron, bamboo (arundinaria), ferns, fuchsia and hydrangea; mature beeches, oaks, pines and larches. Teas at Lochalsh House. On the shores of Loch Alsh, signposted off A87, 3 miles east of Kyle of Lochalsh.
Admission £1.00 Children 50p
SATURDAYS 14th MAY & 23rd JULY 1 – 5.30 pm.
40% to NTS Threave Bursary Fund
For other opening details see Page 141

NOVAR, Evanton
(Mr & Mrs A B L Munro Ferguson)
Water garden and walled garden. Small loch with wild fowl. Teas. Plant stall. Evanton 1½ miles.
Admission £1.50 Children & OAPs 50p
SUNDAY 29th MAY 2 – 6 pm
40% to Riding for the Disabled, Highland branch

SCATWELL, Marybank, Muir of Ord ♿
(Mr & Mrs Robin Fremantle)
Extensive lawns, walled gardens with fine herbaceous borders, greenhouse, water garden and woodland and rock face walks containing rhododendrons, azaleas and many fine trees and shrubs. Home made teas. Produce and craft stalls. Route: Turn off A835 Ullapool road on to A832 signposted Muir of Ord and Beauly. At Marybank turn right up single track road. Beautiful scenic five mile drive to Scatwell.
Admission £1.50
SUNDAY 7th AUGUST 2 – 6 pm
40% to Retinitis Pigmentosa Society

SEA VIEW, Durnamuck, Dundonnell ♿
(Simone & Ian Nelson)
Half acre cottage garden with good views down Little Loch Broom, taken over in September 1989 and compulsively gardened since to provide a wide variety of spring bulbs, plants and shrubs – and expanding. Sorry no dogs. Limited parking. Small gallery – Ian Nelson's watercolours – and some local woodturning. Plant stall. Teas available at Dundonnell Hotel, 6 miles away. Turn towards little Loch Broom, off the main A832 Dundonnell/Gairloch road at Badcaul sign, approx. 1 mile through Badcaul and Durnamuck turning right 400 yards past the Post Office. First house on the left, solar panels on roof.
Admission £1.00 Children free with adults
OPEN EASTER to MID-OCTOBER 10 am – dusk
20% to Dundonnell Village Hall
20% to Cancer Relief Macmillan Fund

TOURNAIG, Poolewe ♿ (partly)
(Sir John Horlick)
Woodland, herbaceous and water garden. Plant stall. Model soldiers can be seen on request – 50p. Tea in house. 1½ miles north of Poolewe on main road. Can be viewed at any time on request.
Admission £1.50 Children under 12 free
WEDNESDAYS 1st JUNE and 3rd AUGUST 2 – 6 pm
20% to St John's Ambulance
20% to Scottish Downs Syndrome Association

ROXBURGH
(BORDERS REGION)

District Organiser:	**Mrs M D Blacklock,** Stable House, Maxton, St Boswells TD6 0EX
Area Organisers:	**The Hon Moyra Campbell,** Scraesburgh, Jedburgh TD8 6QR
Hon. Treasurer:	**Mr D D Gillespie,** Bank of Scotland, Newton St Boswells TD6 0PG

DATES OF OPENING

Floors Castle, Kelso .... Easter weekend and 24 – 28 April,
May, June, September: Sunday to Thursday.
July, August: Open daily
October: Sunday & Wednesday   10.30am – 4.30pm

Monteviot, Jedburgh	Sunday 10 April	2 – 5pm
Newton Don, Kelso	Sunday 15 May	11.30am – 5pm
Mertoun, St Boswells	Sunday 5 June	2 – 6pm
Teviot Water Garden	Saturday 18 June	6 – 8pm
Benrig, Benrig Cottage, Mansfield House & Stable House, St Boswells	Sunday 26 June	2 – 6pm
Corbet Tower, Morebattle	Sunday 10 July	2 – 6pm
Monteviot, Jedburgh	Sunday 17 July	2 – 5pm
Yetholm Village Gardens	Sunday 7 August	2 – 6pm

BENRIG COTTAGE, St Boswells   🛆
(Mrs J E Triscott)
A small garden recently planted with great enthusiasm incorporating roses, herbaceous plants and a small vegetable area. JOINT OPENING WITH BENRIG, MANSFIELD HOUSE and STABLE HOUSE SITUATED ON THE SAME ROAD. Plant stall and cream teas available at Stable House. Parking at Benrig and Mansfield House for all four gardens. St Boswells: two minutes from A68 on the A699 to Kelso.
Admission £2.00, includes all gardens. Children under 14 free.
SUNDAY 26th JUNE 2 – 6 pm
20% to Multiple Sclerosis Society (Borders branch)
20% to St Boswells Parish Church

BENRIG, St Boswells   🛆
(Mr & Mrs Nigel Houldsworth)
Semi-walled garden with shrub roses and herbaceous plants. Magnificent views of the River Tweed. Play area for toddlers. Cake stall. JOINT OPENING WITH BENRIG COTTAGE, STABLE HOUSE and MANSFIELD HOUSE, SITUATED ON THE SAME ROAD. Plant stall and cream teas available at Stable House. Parking at Benrig and Mansfield House for all four gardens. St Boswells: 2 minutes from A68 on the A699 to Kelso.
Admission £2.00, includes all gardens. Children under 14 free.
SUNDAY 26th JUNE 2 – 6 pm
20% to Multiple Sclerosis Society (Borders branch)
20% to St Boswells Parish Church

CORBET TOWER, Morebattle
(Mr & Mrs G H Waddell)
Scottish baronial house (1896) set in parkland in foothills of the Cheviots. Garden includes formal parterre with old fashioned roses and walled garden with herbaceous borders and vegetables. Teas. Plant stall. From A68 Jedburgh road take A698, at Eckford B6401 to Morebattle, then road marked Hownam.
Admission £1.50 Children under 14 free OAPs £1.00
SUNDAY 10th JULY 2 – 6 pm
40% to British Red Cross (Borders branch)

FLOORS CASTLE, Kelso   🛆
(The Duke of Roxburghe)
Floors Castle is situated in beautiful Borders country, overlooking Kelso and the River Tweed. Extensive gardens, grounds and children's play area. Ample parking facilities. Garden Centre & Coffee Shop open daily 10.30 am – 5.30 pm; also Castle, grounds & restaurant. (Last admission to House 4.45 pm). Nearest town Kelso.
Open EASTER WEEKEND, 24th – 28th APRIL, MAY, JUNE, SEPTEMBER: Sundays to Thursdays.
JULY & AUGUST: Open daily. OCTOBER: Sundays & Wednesdays,
10.30am – 4.30 pm.
Donation to Scotland's Gardens Scheme

MANSFIELD HOUSE, St Boswells
(Mr & Mrs D M Forsyth)
18th century manse sitting in one acre of established garden, containing mixed planting of trees, shrubs and clematis. Interesting traditional vegetable garden. JOINT OPENING WITH BENRIG, BENRIG COTTAGE and STABLE HOUSE SITUATED ON THE SAME ROAD. Plant stall and cream teas available at Stable House. Parking at Benrig and Mansfield House for all four gardens. St Boswells: 2 minutes from A68 on the A699 to Kelso.
Admission £2.00, includes all gardens. Children under 14 free.
SUNDAY 26th JUNE 2 – 6 pm
20% to Multiple Sclerosis Society (Borders branch)
20% to St Boswells Parish Church

MERTOUN, St Boswells &
(Duke of Sutherland)
House built by Sir William Scott of Harden in 1703 to the design of Sir William Bruce. Remodelled 1956 by Ian G Lindsay, reducing house to original size. Shrubs, azaleas, herbaceous borders, ornamental pond, etc. View of the River Tweed. Home-made teas. Jedburgh branch British Legion Pipe Band. Plant stall, raffle, cake stall, various other stalls, sideshows, etc. St Boswells 2 miles. Driving south on the A68, turn left opposite The Buccleuch Arms Hotel, continue through village and on for about three-quarters of a mile over River Tweed to first drive on the right.
Admission £1.00 Children under 12 free
SUNDAY 5th JUNE 2 – 6 pm
40% to Mertoun Kirk

MONTEVIOT, Jedburgh
Monteviot stands on a rise above the River Teviot overlooking the rolling Borders countryside. Walled rose garden, shrub and herbaceous borders, water garden of islands linked by bridges, collection of rare trees in pinery. Car park free. Dogs on lead. St Boswells 5 miles, Jedburgh 4 miles. Turn off A68 on to B6400 to Nisbet. Entrance second turning on right.
Admission £1.50 Children under 14 free OAPs 70p
SUNDAY 10th APRIL 2 – 5 pm Daffodil Day. Bunches for sale. Refreshments.
SUNDAY 17th JULY 2 – 5 pm Rose Day. Jedforest Instrumental Band. Children's activities. Cream teas in house. Stalls, including cakes, plants and bottle tombola.
20% to St Mary's Church, Jedburgh
20% to Age Concern (Scotland)

NEWTON DON, Kelso & in parts
(Mr & Mrs William Balfour)
The garden and policies form part of a landscape, believed to have been designed in the 1760s, which is in the midst of a programme of reclamation, replanning and replanting. Come and enjoy acres of fine trees, wonderful views and walks among the bluebells or along the River Eden. The house, a Grade A listed building completed in 1820, will be open. Refreshments, live music, cake stall, plant stall and raffle. If the weather is fine, come early and bring a picnic. Please enter from A6089 Kelso/Gordon road.
Admission £1.50 Children under 10 free
SUNDAY 15th MAY 11.30am – 5 pm
40% to Save the Children (Borders branch)

STABLE HOUSE, St Boswells ♿
(Lt Col & Mrs M D Blacklock)
House converted in 1982 and garden started in 1983. "A plant lovers garden. Here, in an informal design, unusual plants are combined with old fashioned roses, shrubs and herbaceous plants to give colour and interest all summer. All in half an acre; also a courtyard garden with tender climbers, small vegetable garden incorporated into mixed border and newly extended gold border." JOINT OPENING WITH BENRIG, BENRIG COTTAGE AND MANSFIELD HOUSE SITUATED ON THE SAME ROAD. Home made cream teas in Garden Room and Conservatory. Plant stall. Cake stall and raffle. Parking at Benrig and Mansfield House for all four gardens. St Boswells: two minutes from A68 on the A699 to Kelso.
Admission £2.00, includes all gardens. Children under 14 free.
SUNDAY 26th JUNE 2 – 6 pm
20% to Multiple Sclerosis (Borders branch)
20% to St Boswells Parish Church

 # TEVIOT WATER GARDEN, Eckford, Kelso
(Mr & Mrs D B Wilson)
A water garden falling down to the River Teviot. Terraced with ponds and waterfalls and a wide range of interesting planting combining bog and water plants with shrubs, herbaceous and roses. Plant stall. Wine. Between Kelso and Jedburgh on A698.
Admission £1.50 Under 15 free.
SATURDAY 18th JUNE 6 – 8 pm
40% to British Red Cross (Borders branch)

YETHOLM VILLAGE GARDENS

2 GRAFTON COURT (Mr George Lee) ♿
Colourful garden filled with many different plants. Mr Lee's collection of dahlias can be seen in his allotment close by.

25 WOODBANK ROAD (Mr & Mrs Burnett)
The garden has been carefully designed to combine shrubs and colourful bedding plants. It has won the village council garden competition for the past ten years.

IVY HOUSE (Mr & Mrs Patterson) ♿
Walled garden to rear of house with herbaceous border, fruit trees, heathers, hanging baskets and a pond.

8 THE YETT (Mr & Mrs R Begg)
Wonderful situation overlooking the Bowmont valley. A garden and small scree area filled with interesting alpines, mainly propagated by owners.

Four gardens situated in Yetholm Village at the foot of the Cheviot Hills. The village has ample parking and tickets will be sold on the village green. Kelso 17½ miles. Wooler 13½ miles. Jedburgh 14 miles.
Admission £1.50, includes all gardens. Children over 14 & OAPs £1.00
SUNDAY 7th AUGUST 2 – 6 pm
20% to St Columba's Hospice, Edinburgh
20% to RNIB Talking Books Service

STEWARTRY OF KIRKCUDBRIGHT
(DUMFRIES & GALLOWAY REGION)

District Organiser:	**Mrs J I Gillespie,** Danevale Park, Crossmichael, Castle Douglas DG7 2LP
Area Organisers:	**Miss P Bain,** Annick Bank, Hardgate, Castle Douglas
	Mrs C Cathcart, Culraven, Borgue, Kirkcudbright DG6 4SG
	Mrs A Chandler, Auchenvin, Rockcliffe, Dumfries
	Mrs Jane Hannay, Kirklandhill, Kirkpatrick Durham, Castle Douglas
	Mrs Brenda Ledward, Kingarth, New Abbey DG2 8DH
	Mrs W J McCulloch, Ardwall, Gatehouse of Fleet DG7 2EN
	Mrs C A Ramsay, Limits, St Johns, Dalry, Castle Douglas DG7 3SW
Hon. Treasurer:	**Mr W Little,** 54 St Andrew Street, Castle Douglas DG7 1EN

DATES OF OPENING

Danevale Park, Crossmichael	Sunday 20 February	2 – 5pm
Roughhills, Sandyhills	Sunday 1 May	2 – 5pm
Barnhourie Mill, Colvend, Dalbeattie	Sunday 15 May	2 – 5pm
Dromineen, Gatehouse of Fleet	Sunday 22 May	2 – 5pm
Corsock House, Castle Douglas	Sunday 29 May	2 – 5pm
		also open by appointment
Walton Park, Castle Douglas	Sunday 29 May	2.30 – 5pm
Hensol, Mossdale	Sunday 5 June	2 – 5pm
Cally Gardens, Gatehouse of Fleet	Sunday 19 June	10am – 5.30pm
Southwick House, Dumfries	Sunday 26 June	2 – 5pm
	27 June – 3 July	afternoons
Balmaclellan House, nr New Galloway	Sunday 3 July	2 – 5pm
Argrennan House, Castle Douglas	Sunday 17 July	2 – 5pm
Spottes, Haugh-of-Urr	Sunday 24 July	2 – 5pm
Threave School of Gardening	Sunday 7 August	9am – 5.30pm
Cally Gardens, Gatehouse of Fleet	Sunday 14 August	10am – 5.30pm

ARGRENNAN HOUSE, Castle Douglas ♿
(Robert Reddaway & Tulane Kidd)
Georgian house set in beautiful parkland with specimen trees. A large walled garden with traditional herbaceous borders, shrub borders and rose garden. Water garden with box parterres and 1840 rockery. Woodland walks. Water garden, ponds and bog gardens. Teas served in old kitchen. House not open. Route: Castle Douglas 3½ miles. Kirkcudbright 3½ miles on A711.
Admission £1.50 Children 50p
SUNDAY 17th JULY 2 – 5 pm
40% to Crossroads (Stewartry branch)

BALMACLELLAN HOUSE, near New Galloway ♿
(Mr & Mrs Ian Douglas)
A good mixed garden, both formal and informal, with well established shrubs and trees, especially magnolias and azaleas. Plant stall. Teas under cover. Route: 12 miles from Castle Douglas, turn off A713 at Ken Bridge Hotel, follow yellow signs to garden.
Admission £1.50 Children 50p
SUNDAY 3rd JULY 2 – 5 pm
40% to Crossroads (Stewartry branch)

BARNHOURIE MILL, Colvend, Dalbeattie ♿ **(partly)**
(Dr M R Paton)
Flowering shrubs, dwarf conifers and an especially fine collection of rhododendron species. Tea in house £1. Cars free. Dalbeattie 5 miles. Route A7610 from Dumfries.
Admission £1.50 Children 50p.
SUNDAY 15th MAY 2 – 5pm
40% to Scottish Wildlife Trust

CALLY GARDENS, Gatehouse of Fleet ♿
(Mr Michael Wickenden)
A specialist nursery in a fine 2.7 acre, 18th century walled garden with old vinery and bothy, all surrounded by the Cally Oak woods. Our collection of 3,000 varieties can be seen and many will be available pot-grown, especially rare herbaceous perennials. Forestry nature trails nearby. Route: From Dumfries take the Gatehouse turning off A75 and turn left, through the Cally Palace Hotel Gateway from where the gardens are well signposted.
Voluntary admission charge
SUNDAYS 19th JUNE and 14th AUGUST 10 am – 5.30 pm
40% to Save the Children Fund

CORSOCK HOUSE, Castle Douglas
(Mr & Mrs M L Ingall)
With David Bryce turretted "Scottish Baronial" house at background, rhododendrons, woodland walks with temple, water gardens and loch. Teas by Corsock WRI. Cars free. Dumfries 14 miles, Castle Douglas 10 miles, Corsock ½ mile on A712.
Admission £1.50 Children 50p
SUNDAY 29th MAY 2 – 5 pm. Also open by appointment.
40% to Gardeners' Royal Benevolent Society

DANEVALE PARK, Crossmichael
(Mrs J I Gillespie)
Open for snowdrops. Woodland walks. Tea in house. Route: A713. Crossmichael 1 mile,
Castle Douglas 3 miles.
Admission £1.00
Sunday 20th February 2 – 5 pm
40% to Crossmichael Village Hall

DROMINEEN, Laurieston Road, Gatehouse
(Mrs Longfield)
Good rhododendrons, azaleas and heathers with stream flowing through garden.
Gatehouse of Fleet 2 miles.
Admission £1.50
SUNDAY 22nd MAY 2 – 5 pm
40% to Guide Dogs for the Blind

HENSOL, Mossdale, Castle Douglas &
(Lady Henderson)
An early 19th century granite house designed by Lugar. Established garden surrounding
house. Alpines, shrubs, water garden and new woodland garden. River walks. Plant stall.
Cars free. Tea in house. Route: A762, 3 miles north of Laurieston.
Admission £1.50 Children 50p
SUNDAY 5th JUNE 2 – 5 pm
40% to RNLI

ROUGHHILLS, Sandyhills, Dalbeattie
(Mr & Mrs Ronald Percy)
Rhododendrons, azaleas, camellias and spring flowering shrubs. Teas in house. Plant
stall. Parking at Sandyhills Car Park, transport to garden provided. Dalbeattie 5 miles,
Sandyhills ½ mile, through village on A710 to Dumfries.
Admission £1.50 Children 50p
SUNDAY 1st MAY 2 – 5 pm
40% to Multiple Sclerosis Society (Dumfries branch)

SOUTHWICK HOUSE, Dumfries & (formal garden only)
(Mrs C H Thomas)
Formal garden with lily ponds and herbaceous borders, shrubs, vegetables, fruit and
greenhouse. Water garden with boating pond, lawns and fine trees, through which flows
the Southwick burn. Tea & biscuits, ice cream and soft drinks. On A710, near
Caulkerbush. Dalbeattie 7 miles, Dumfries 17 miles.
Admission £1.50 Children 50p
SUNDAY 26th JUNE 2 – 5 pm 27th June – 3rd July, every afternoon with honesty box.
40% to Soldiers', Sailors' & Airmen's Families Association

SPOTTES, Haugh-of-Urr &
(Sir Michael & Lady Herries)
Walled garden with yew hedges and flower beds. Woodland and pondside walks; old
trees and lawns. Teas. Plant stalls. Haugh-of-Urr ¼ mile, Castle Douglas 4 miles.
Admission £1.50 Children 50p OAPs £1.00
SUNDAY 24th JULY 2 – 5 pm
20% to Girl Guides
20% to Save the Children

THREAVE SCHOOL OF GARDENING, Castle Douglas &

(The National Trust for Scotland)

Baronial house by Peddie & Kinnear. 60 acres of garden. Ornamental, fruit, vegetable and glasshouses. House not open. Plant stall. Route: A75, one mile west of Castle Douglas.

Admission £3.00 Children & OAPs £1.50

SUNDAY 7th AUGUST 9 am – 5.30 pm

40% to NTS Threave Bursary Fund

For other opening details see Page 140

WALTON PARK, Castle Douglas &

(Mr Jeremy Brown)

Early 19th century double bow-fronted house with later additions. Walled garden, gentian border. Flowering shrubs, rhododendrons and azaleas. Cars free. Tea in house. Plant stall. Route: B974, 3½ miles from A75.

Admission £1.50 Children 50p

SUNDAY 29th MAY 2.30 – 5 pm

40% to Carnsalloch Cheshire Home

TWEEDDALE
(BORDERS REGION)

District Organiser:	**Mrs K St C Cunningham,** Hallmanor, Peebles EH45 9JN
Area Organisers:	**Mrs D Balfour-Scott,** Langlawhill, Broughton, Lanarkshire ML12 6HL
	Mrs R K Brown, Runic Cross, Waverley Road, Innerleithen EH44 6QH
	Mrs H B Marshall, Baddinsgill, West Linton, Innerleithen
Hon. Treasurer:	**Mr K St C Cunningham,** Hallmanor, Peebles EH45 9JN

DATES OF OPENING

Kailzie Gardens, Peebles .... Daily 25 March – 30 October   11 – 5.30pm

Netherurd House, Blyth Bridge .... Sunday 24 April   2 – 6pm

Dawyck Botanic Garden .... Sunday 8 May   10am – 6pm

Haystoun, Peebles .... Sunday 29 May   2 – 5.30pm

Hallmanor, Kirkton Manor .... Sunday 5 June   2 – 6pm

Stobo Water Garden, Peebles .... Sunday 12 June   2 – 6pm

Cringletie House Hotel, Eddleston .... Sat & Sun 25/26 June   2 – 5pm

Portmore, Eddleston .... Sunday 24 July   2 – 5pm

Quarter House, Broughton .... Sunday 24 July   2 – 6pm

CRINGLETIE HOUSE HOTEL, Eddleston &

(Mr & Mrs S L Maguire)

House by David Bryce. Former home of Wolfe Murray family, set in 28 acres of woodlands, including walled garden which includes fruit trees, vegetables, etc. Herbaceous borders. Croquet demonstration by Scottish Croquet Association. Tea 3.30 – 4.30 pm. Cars free. Peebles 2½ miles. Donation box. Bus: No. 62 Edinburgh/Peebles. Hotel signposted from A703 Edinburgh/Peebles. SGS signs.

SATURDAY 25th JUNE 2 – 5 pm
40% to St Columba's Hospice
SUNDAY 26th JUNE 2 – 5 pm
40% to Royal Blind Asylum & School

DAWYCK BOTANIC GARDEN, Stobo & (limited access)

(Specialist Garden of the Royal Botanic Garden, Edinburgh)

Arboretum of rare trees, rhododendrons and shrubs. Terraces and stonework constructed by Italian landscape gardeners in 1820. Guided tours. Guide dogs only. 8 miles south of Peebles on B712. SGS signs.

Admission £1.00

SUNDAY 8th MAY 10 am – 6 pm
40% to Royal Botanic Gardens, Edinburgh
For other opening details see page 126

HALLMANOR, Kirkton Manor, Peebles

(Mr & Mrs K St C Cunningham)

Rhododendrons and azaleas, primulas, wooded grounds with loch and salmon ladder. 800 ft above sea level in the Manor valley. Teas. Plant stall. Peebles 6 miles. Off A72 Peebles/Glasgow road.

Admission £1.00 Children free

SUNDAY 5th JUNE 2 – 6 pm
40% to Manor Church

HAYSTOUN, Peebles & (partly)

(Mr & Mrs D Coltman)

16th century house (not open). Walled garden, recently planted wild garden. Plant stall. Teas. Dogs on lead only please. A703 Edinburgh/Peebles, over Tweed bridge in Peebles, follow SGS signs for 1½ miles.

Admission £1.00 Children free

SUNDAY 29th MAY 2 – 5.30 pm
40% to St Columba's Hospice

KAILZIE GARDENS, Peebles &

(Lady Buchan-Hepburn)

Semi-formal walled garden with rose garden, herbaceous borders and old fashioned roses. Greenhouses. Woodland and burnside walks among massed spring bulbs and, later, rhododendrons and azaleas. Wild garden set in beautiful Tweed valley amid fine old trees. Newly opened reservoir fishing. Free car park. Picnic area. Children's play corner. Home-made teas in licensed restaurant. Plant Centre. Art gallery and shop. Parties by arrangment.

Admission: March to mid-May & October, Adults £1.50 Children 5 – 14 50p; mid-May to end September, Adults £2.00 Children 5 – 14 50p

OPEN DAILY 25th MARCH – 30th OCTOBER 11 am – last entry 5.30 pm.
Donation to Scotland's Gardens Scheme

NETHERURD HOUSE, Blyth Bridge &

(Girl Guides Association, Scotland)
Delightful setting with views towards Wether Law. Extensive lawns. Rediscovered Victorian rock garden under restoration. Spring daffodils. Adventure trail. Easy paths and woodland walks. Tea with home baking. Plant stall. Raffle. Cars free. Just west of Blyth Bridge on A721. Follow SGS signs.
Admission £1.00 Children 50p
SUNDAY 24th APRIL 2 – 6 pm
40% to Girl Guides Association, Scotland (Netherurd Training Centre)

PORTMORE, Eddleston
(Mr & Mrs D H L Reid)
Walled garden with herbaceous borders, herb garden, ornamental vegetable garden, greenhouses with Victorian grotto. Newly planted shrub and rose garden and parterre. Plant stall. Cream teas. Dogs on lead. Edinburgh to Peebles bus No. 62.
Admission £1.00
SUNDAY 24th JULY 2 – 5 pm
40% to Crossroads Care Scheme

QUARTER HOUSE, Broughton
(Mrs Jenny Browning OBE)
Hill garden, with beautiful mature trees, overlooking the Holms Water and hills of Upper Tweeddale. Herbaceous borders, fine hedges, pond and woodland walks. Cake and candy stall. Plant stall. Teas. Cars free. Bus route A701 Edinburgh/Moffat. 2 miles south of Broughton.
Admission £1.00
SUNDAY 24th JULY 2 – 6 pm
40% to British Red Cross Society (Glasgow & Renfrewshire Branch)

STOBO WATER GARDEN, Stobo, Peebles
(Mr Hugh Seymour)
Water garden, lakes, azaleas and rhododendrons. Woodland walks. Cars free. Cream teas in village hall. Peebles 7 miles, signposted on B712 Lyne/Broughton road.
Admission £1.00 Children free
SUNDAY 12th JUNE 2 – 6 pm
20% to Stobo Kirk
20% to Save the Children Fund

WIGTOWN
(DUMFRIES & GALLOWAY REGION)

District Organiser:	**Mrs Francis Brewis,** Ardwell House, Stranraer DG9 9LY
Area Organisers:	**Mrs Andrew Gladstone,** Craichlaw, Kirkcowan, Newton Stewart DG8 0DQ
Hon. Treasurer:	**Mr G S Fleming,** Bank of Scotland, 64 George Street, Stranraer DG9 7JN

DATES OF OPENING

Ardwell House Gardens, Ardwell .... Daily 1 March – 31 October   10am – 6pm

Castle Kennedy & Lochinch Gardens,
  Stranraer .... Daily 1 April – 30 September   10am – 5pm

Galloway House Gardens, Garlieston .... Daily 1 March – 31 October   9am – 5pm

Whitehills, Newton Stewart .... 1 April – 31 October   by appointment

Ardwell House Gardens, Ardwell .... Sunday 1 May   2 – 5pm

Glenwhan, Dunragit .... Sunday 15 May   10am – 5pm

Logan, Port Logan .... Sunday 29 May   10am – 6pm

Logan Botanic Garden, Port Logan .... Sunday 29 May   10am – 6pm

Whitehills, Newton Stewart .... Sunday 5 June   2 – 5pm

Bargaly House, Palnure .... Sunday 19 June   2 – 5pm

ARDWELL HOUSE GARDENS, Ardwell, Stranraer

(Mrs Faith Brewis and Mr Francis Brewis)
Daffodils, spring flowers, rhododendrons, flowering shrubs, coloured foliage and rock plants. Moist garden at smaller pond and a walk round larger ponds, with views over Luce Bay. Plants for sale and self-pick fruit in season. Collection box. House not open. Dogs welcome on leads. Picnic site on shore. Teas available in Ardwell village. Stranraer 10 miles. Route A76 towards Mull of Galloway. (Walled garden and greenhouses close at 5 pm March, April and May.)
Admission £1.50 Children & OAPs 50p
DAILY 1st MARCH to 31st OCTOBER 10 am – 6 pm
Donation to Scotland's Gardens Scheme
SUNDAY 1st MAY 2 – 5 pm
40% to Save the Children Fund

BARGALY HOUSE, Palnure, Newton Stewart &

(Mr Jonathan Bradburn)
Unusual trees and shrubs in extensive borders, rock and water garden, walled garden with large herbaceous border. Woodland and river walks. Refreshments available. Palnure 2 miles, A75. Bus stop, Palnure.
Admission £1.00 Children 50p
SUNDAY 19th JUNE 2 – 5 pm
Donation to Scotland's Gardens Scheme

CASTLE KENNEDY & LOCHINCH GARDENS, Stranraer &

(The Earl and Countess of Stair)
The gardens are laid out on a peninsula betwen two lochs and extend to 75 acres from the ruined Castle Kennedy to Lochinch Castle. They are world famous for rhododendrons, azaleas, magnolias and embothriums and contain specimens from Hooker and other expeditions. Choice of peaceful walks. Plant centre. Gift shop with refreshments.
Admission charged. 20% discount for parties over 30 people. Cars and disabled free. Stranraer 5 miles on A75. For further information telephone 0776 – 702024.
DAILY 1st APRIL – 30th SEPTEMBER 10 am – 5 pm
Donation to Scotland's Gardens Scheme

GALLOWAY HOUSE GARDENS, Garlieston &

(Galloway House Gardens Trust)
Garden created in 1740 by Lord Garlies, eldest son of 6th Earl of Galloway, later owned by Sir Malcolm McEacharn, whose son, Neil, created the garden at the Villa Taranto on Lake Maggiore, Italy. Rhododendrons, shrubs, fine trees, snowdrops and daffodils in early spring. Greenhouses and camellia house (March/April) in walled garden, eucryphias in late summer. Many of the recent additions to the gardens were suggested by the late Mr & Mrs Strutt who were gifted gardeners. Admission by collection box. Home-made teas in Garlieston village, half a mile. Sandy bay for picnics and bathing in sea. Route: follow signs from Garlieston.
Admission £1.00 OAPs 50p Families £2.50
OPEN 1st MARCH – 31st OCTOBER 9 am – 5 pm (Walled garden until 4.30 pm).
40% to Sorbie Church Organ Fund

GLENWHAN, Dunragit, Stranraer ♿
(Mr & Mrs William Knott)
A hilltop garden with splendid views of Luce Bay. Trees, shrubs, rock and water gardens in natural landscape round two lochans. Car park free. No dogs except guide dogs, please. Lunches and refreshments available. Plant stall.
Admission £1.50 Children under 14 50p
SUNDAY 15th MAY 10 am – 5 pm
40% to Save the Children Fund

LOGAN BOTANIC GARDEN, Port Logan, by Stranraer ♿
(Specialist Garden of the Royal Botanic Garden, Edinburgh)
One of the most exotic gardens in Britain. Magnificent Tree ferns and Cabbage palms grow within a walled garden together with other southern hemisphere plants. Colourful herbaceous borders. Free guided tours of summer colour throughout the day; special access to the grounds of Logan House. Salad Bar open 10 am – 6 pm. Route: 10 miles south of Stranraer on A716, then 2½ miles from Ardwell village.
Admission £1.50 Children 50p Concessions £1.00
SUNDAY 29th MAY 10 am – 6 pm
40% to Royal Botanic Garden, Edinburgh
For other opening details see page 123

LOGAN, Port Logan, by Stranraer ♿
(The Trustees of Sir Ninian Buchan-Hepburn)
Queen Anne house, 1701. Addition by David Bryce 1874, removed 1949. Rare exotic tropical plants and shrubs. Fine specie and hybrid rhododendrons. Route: 10 miles south of Stranraer on A716, then 1½ miles from Ardwell village.
Admission £1.50 Children 50p Concessions £1.00
SUNDAY 29th MAY 10 am – 6 pm
40% to Port Logan Hall Fund

WHITEHILLS, Newton Stewart ♿
(Mr & Mrs C A Weston)
Rhododendrons, azaleas, heathers and many exotic shrubs. Scree, water and winter gardens. Woodland walks. Rhododendron and shrub nursery. Plant stall. Tea. Dogs on lead only. Ample parking. Newton Stewart 1 mile. Wood of Cree road ¼ mile north of Minnigaff Church (signposted to RSPB reserve).
Admission £1.50 Accompanied children under 14 free
SUNDAY 5th JUNE 2 – 5 pm
Open by appointment from 1st April to 31st October Tel: 0671 402049
40% to Friends of Newton Stewart Hospital

ROYAL BOTANIC GARDEN EDINBURGH

One of the world's great botanical institutions – an internationally renowned centre for plant science research, education and conservation, whose unique living collections are displayed for visitors in 4 remarkable gardens at Edinburgh, Benmore, Logan and Dawyck.

FRIENDS *of the*
ROYAL BOTANIC GARDEN EDINBURGH

The Friends organisation was founded in 1991 to support the Garden by taking an active interest in its work.

The Friends receive a regular newsletter and can participate in a lively programme of lectures, guided walks, garden visits and plant sales.

They have already made valuable contributions towards Garden plant-collecting expeditions and visitor developments.

Join the Friends — share in the great tradition of the Garden! The subscription is £15, or £20 for a family, per annum. Please write or call the Friends Office, Royal Botanic Garden, Edinburgh EH3 5LR. Tel. 031-552 5339.

ROYAL BOTANIC GARDEN EDINBURGH

Inverleith Row, Edinburgh.

Lothian. Off A902, 1m N of city centre.

Scotland's national Botanic Garden contains a unique collection of plants from throughout the world in a beautiful landscaped setting. It is especially famous for its large rock garden and ten landscaped glasshouses. Other features of interest include a demonstration garden, peat garden, woodland garden and arboretum, and alpine courtyard. Full exhibition and education programme, including Garden Guide Tours.

Botanics Shop with Plant Sales; Terrace Cafe; Admission free.

Open Daily (except Christmas and New Year's Day).
*   10 am - 4 pm November to February.*
*   10 am - 6 pm March to April.*
*   10 am - 8 pm May to August.*
*   10 am - 6 pm September to October.*

Royal Botanic Garden, Inverleith Row, Edinburgh EH3 5LR.
Telephone: 031-552 7171.   Fax: 031-552 0382.

Royal Botanic Garden Edinburgh

YOUNGER BOTANIC GARDEN BENMORE

Argyll. On A815, 7m N of Dunoon.

This magnificent garden, set amid the hills of the Eachaig Valley contains some of the tallest trees in Britain, including a famous Giant Redwood avenue, which is higher than eight double-decked buses. It also has a splendid collection of over 250 species of rhododendrons and many other plants from the Himalayas. Spring to early summer is the best time for enjoying the flowering shrubs, while in September and October there is a fine display of autumn colours.

Restaurant and Botanics Shop with Plant Sales.

Garden open daily, 15 March to 31 October inclusive, 10 am to 6 pm (and at other times by arrangement).

Admission £1.50 adults, £1.00 concessions, 50p children.
Facilities for the disabled. Dogs permitted on a short lead.

Younger Botanic Garden, Benmore, Dunoon, Argyll PA23 8QU.
Telephone: 0369 6261.   Fax: 0369 6369.

Royal Botanic Garden Edinburgh

LOGAN BOTANIC GARDEN

Wigtownshire. On B7065, 14m S of Stranraer.

This is undoubtedly one of the most exotic gardens in Britain. Surrounded by the warming influence of the Gulf Stream, warm temperate plants, including magnificent tree ferns and palms, flourish out of doors. Inside the old walled gardens there are many unusual plants from the Southern Hemisphere. Of special interest are the fine water gardens, peat walls, gunnera bog and the wealth of scented trees and shrubs.

Salad Bar and Botanics Shop with Plant Sales.

Garden Open daily, 15 March to 31 October inclusive, 10 am to 6 pm (and at other times by arrangement).

Admission £1.50 adults, £1.00 concessions, 50p children.

**Special Scotland's Gardens Scheme Opening
SUNDAY 29 MAY—10 am to 6 pm.**

Free Guided Tours, and special access to Logan House Gardens. Admission £1.50 (60% to SGS).

Logan Botanic Garden, Port Logan, Stranraer, Wigtownshire DG9 9ND. Telephone: 0776 860231.   Fax: 0776 860333.

Royal Botanic Garden Edinburgh

DAWYCK BOTANIC GARDEN

Stobo, Peebles-shire. On B712, 8m SW of Peebles.

This historic arboretum, overlooking the beautiful Tweed Valley, contains trees which are over 300 years old. Some of the conifers are 40m tall and still growing strong. There is also a very good collection of rhododendrons and in spring large areas are carpeted with daffodils. Many people visit Dawyck at the end of the season to see the spectacular autumn colours. The arboretum and surrounding mature woodland are rich in wildlife.

Conservatory Shop with Light Refreshments.

Garden open daily, 15 March to 22 October, 10 am to 6 pm (and at other times by arrangement).

Admission £1.00 adults, 50p children and concessions.

**Special Scotland's Gardens Scheme Opening
SUNDAY 8 MAY—10 am to 6 pm.**

Free Guided Tours.   Admission £1.00 (60% to SGS).

**Dawyck Botanic Garden, Stobo, Peebles-shire EH45 9JU.
Telephone: 0721 760254.   Fax: 0721 760214.**

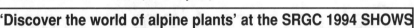

GARDENS IN TRUST

THE NATIONAL TRUST FOR SCOTLAND opens the gates to a galaxy of some of Scotland's finest gardens for you.

From Threave in the south, to Inverewe in the north, the Trust cares for a wide variety of gardens. Some are designed by and are for the specialist while others are simply gardens of great beauty.

In all of them you can relax and appreciate the care that goes into their presentation. A selection of the gardens of the National Trust for Scotland is described in the following twelve pages.

Although Trust gardens are open most days of the year, active support is given to Scotland's Gardens Scheme by designated special days during the year when our gardens are open under the scheme. All the appropriate dates and opening times are listed in this booklet.

ANNUAL LECTURE

The National Trust for Scotland's annual horticultural lecture in association with the Royal Botanic Garden will be given this year in Edinburgh on 14 September by Professor Ghillean T Prance, Director of Royal Kew Botanic Gardens. Professor Prance will give an illustrated lecture on "The Flowers of the Amazon Forest and their Conservation". As usual, the lecture will be preceded by expert-led tours of the Royal Botanic Garden, Edinburgh, followed by a boxed lunch with wine to the accompaniment of flute and piano music. All-inclusive tickets for this very popular annual "Botanics Day", priced £13 are available from Trust headquarters at 5 Charlotte Square, Edinburgh EH2 4DU.

Arduaine Garden

**Argyll. On A816, 20 miles from
Oban and Lochgilphead**

Branklyn Garden

**Tayside.
A85, Dundee Road, Perth**

THIS ATTRACTIVE plantsman's garden at Arduaine occupies a spectacular site overlooking Loch Melfort. It has a superb collection of rhododendrons and specimen trees. Some of these are of remarkable size.

The early garden was of simple, formal design with shelter belts of mixed woodland. Between 1922 and 1929 this garden was developed. In 1971, brothers Harry and Edmund Wright bought the garden and began restoration and improvement. In 1992 they presented the garden to the Trust.

Open all year, daily 9.30 a.m.—sunset. Admission: adults £2.00, children £1.00, adult parties £1.60, schools 80p.

Free entry for The National Trust for Scotland Members.

ON A PERTH HILLSIDE, looking southward over the Tay, Branklyn has been described as "the finest two acres of private garden in the country". An outstanding collection of plants, particularly of alpines, was made by the late Mr and Mrs John Renton. Mr Renton bequeathed the garden to the Trust with an endowment. The Trust agreed to accept the garden because of its great worth—a decision made possible because of generous assistance from the City of Perth.

Open 1 March to 23 October, daily 9.30 a.m.—sunset. Admission: adults £2.00, children £1.00, adult parties £1.60, schools 80p.

Free entry for The National Trust for Scotland Members.

Brodick Castle, Garden and Country Park

Isle of Arran, Strathclyde. (Ferry from Ardrossan (and Kintyre in summer)

BRODICK CASTLE and its gardens on the Isle of Arran came into the care of the Trust in 1958 following the death of the Duchess of Montrose, whose home it was. She created a woodland garden, considered one of the finest rhododendron gardens in Europe. Plants from Himalaya, Burma and China flourish in the gentle west coast climate and give a continuous display of colour from January to August. The formal garden is 250 years old and has recently been restored as a Victorian garden. A country park was established in 1980 through an agreement between Cunninghame District Council and the Trust.

Special nature trail for disabled. Wheelchairs available. Braille sheets.

Open: Castle, Good Friday to Easter Monday and 1 May to 30 September, daily 1 – 5; 9 to 30 April and 1 to 23 October, Saturday/Sunday 1 – 5 (last admission 4.30). Reception Centre, restaurant and shop (dates as castle), 10 – 4.30. Garden and Country Park, all year, daily 9.30 – sunset.

GOATFELL: open all year.

Admission: Castle and garden, adults £4.00, children £2.00, adult parties £3.20, schools £1.60. Garden only, adults £2.00, children £1.00. Car park free. Ferry from Ardrossan (55 minutes) to Brodick. Connecting bus, pier to castle (2 miles). Ferry enquiries to Caledonian MacBrayne: tel. Gourock (0475) 650100.

Free entry for The National Trust for Scotland Members.

Crathes Castle and Garden

Kincardine and Deeside, Grampian

On A93, 3 miles east of Banchory and 15 miles west of Aberdeen

THE CASTLE AND ITS GARDENS are situated near Banchory, in a delightful part of Royal Deeside. Formerly Crathes was the home of the late Sir James and Lady Burnett of Leys, whose lifelong interests found expression in the gardens and in one of the best collections of trees and shrubs to be found in Britain. Great yew hedges dating from 1702 surround several of the small gardens of which the garden is composed. Given by the late Sir James Burnett of Leys, Bt, in 1951, together with an endowment. Wheelchair access to garden and grounds, trail for disabled, shop, exhibitions, adventure playground, restaurant and invalid toilets. Wheelchairs available.

Open: Castle, Visitor Centre, shop, licensed restaurant and plant sales. 1 April to 23 October, daily 11 – 5.30 (last admission to castle 4.45). Other times by appointment only. Garden and grounds, all year, daily 9.30 – sunset.

Admission: Castle, gardens and ground, adults £4.00, children £2.00, pre-booked adult parties £3.20, children parties £1.60. Grounds only: Adults £1.80, children 90p.

Enquiries and all bookings: tel: Crathes (0330) 844525.

Free entry for The National Trust for Scotland Members.

♛ The National Trust for Scotland
Culzean Castle, Garden and Country Park
Kyle and Carrick, Strathclyde
A719, 4 miles south-west of Maybole and 12 miles south of Ayr

CULZEAN CASTLE AND COUNTRY PARK is the Trust's most visited property and one of the major tourist attractions in Scotland.

The range of interests and activities at Culzean make it a perfect day out for the family. The Fountain Garden lies in front of Robert Adam's magnificent Castle, with terraces and herbaceous borders, reflecting its Georgian elegance.

Scotland's first Country Park, consisting of 563 acres, contains a wealth of interest from shoreline through Deer Park, Swan Pond to mature parklands, gardens, woodland walks and adventure playground. A conservatory has been restored to its former glory as an orangery. Ranger/Naturalists located at Visitor Centre provide excellent services for visitors including many guided walks. An environmental education service and interpretation programme are based on the Country Park.

The Visitor Centre facilities include a shop, licensed self-service restaurant, introductory exhibition to Culzean, auditorium and information. For disabled—lift in castle, toilets, wheelchairs, induction loop for hard of hearing.

Open: Castle, Visitor Centre, licensed self-service restaurant and shops, 1 April to 23 October, daily 10.30 – 5.30 (last tour 5). Other times by appointment. Country Park, all year, daily 9.30 – sunset.

Admission: Castle, adults £3.50, children £1.80; Country Park, adults £3, children £1.50; adult parties £2.50, schools £1.25, school coaches £20. Combined ticket, Castle and Country Park, adults £5.50, children £3.00, adult parties £4.50, schools £2.50.

Enquiries and all party bookings: tel. Kirkoswald (065 56) 269.

Additional charge to non-members at special events in August 1994. Details available from the Principal.

Free entry for The National Trust for Scotland members.

133

Falkland Palace Garden
Fife
A912, 11 miles north of Kirkcaldy

THE ROYAL GARDEN at Falkland Palace in Fife, which the Stuart Kings and Queens of Scotland knew, was restored after the war by the late Keeper, Major Michael Crichton Stuart, M.C., M.A., to a design by Percy Cane. Trees and shrubs and herbaceous borders give a long-lasting display from spring-flowering cherries to the rich autumn colouring of the maples. The greenhouse provides a colourful show during the greater part of the year. Exhibition in Town Hall of the history of the Palace and Royal Burgh of Falkland. Ramp into garden for wheelchairs.

Open: Palace and garden, 1 April to 23 October, Monday – Saturday 11 – 5.30, Sunday 1.30 – 5.30 (last admission to palace 4.30, to garden 5). Town Hall, 1 April to 23 October, daily 1 – 5.30 (last admission 5).

Admission: palace and garden, adults £4.00, children £2.00, adult parties £3.20, children parties £1.60 (these charges include entrance to Town Hall Exhibition). Garden only, adults £2.00, children £1.00: Scots Guards and members of the Scots Guards Association (wearing the Association's badge) admitted free.

Free entry for The National Trust for Scotland Members.

Hill of Tarvit Mansion

Fife. Off A916
2¹/₂ miles south of Cupar

Inveresk Lodge Garden

East Lothian. A6124 south of
Musselburgh, 6 miles east
of Edinburgh

THIS MANSION HOUSE and garden were remodelled by Sir Robert Lorimer in 1906 for Mr F. B. Sharp. Although the garden was developed and consequently changed, much of the original Lorimer design for it remains. The garden is still being developed with the object of creating greater interest and colour during the year. Bequeathed in 1949 by Miss E. C. Sharp.

Tearoom and House open: Good Friday to Easter Monday and 1 May to 23 October, daily 1.30 – 5.30; 9 to 30 April, Saturday/Sunday 1.30 – 5.30 (last admission 4.45). Garden and Grounds, all year, daily 9.30 – sunset.

Admission house and garden, adults £3.00, children £1.50, adult parties £2.40, schools £1.20, garden only (honesty box), adults £1.00, children 50p.

Free entry for The National Trust for Scotland Members.

INVERESK, on the southern fringes of Musselburgh, is one of the most unspoiled villages of the Lothians. The 17th century Lodge (which is not open to the public) is the oldest building in the village. The garden has been almost completely remodelled since the Trust was presented with the property and an endowment, by Mrs Helen E. Brunton in 1959. This reconstruction is rather similar to the garden as it was in 1851. This is a happy coincidence, for the old plan was found after the present layout was completed. There are good examples of shrubs, trees and other plants for smaller gardens

Open: 1 April to 30 September, Monday – Friday 10 – 4.30, Saturday/Sunday 2 – 5, 2 October to 31 March, Monday – Friday 10 – 4.30, Sunday 2– 5.

Admission: adult £1.00 (honesty box).

Free entry for The National Trust for Scotland Members.

Inverewe Garden

Ross and Cromarty, Highland

On A832, by Poolewe, 6 miles north-east of Gairloch

THIS MAGNIFICENT HIGHLAND GARDEN, near Poolewe, is in an impressive setting of mountains, moorland and sea-loch and attracts over 130,000 visitors a year. When it was founded in 1862 by Osgood Mackenzie, only a dwarf willow grew where plants from many lands now flourish in a profusion as impressive as it is unexpected. Planned as a wild garden it includes Australian tree ferns, exotic plants from China, and a magnificent Magnolia campbellii. Given into the care of the Trust in 1952 by Mrs Mairi T. Sawyer, together with an endowment. Disabled access to greenhouse and half paths. Wheelchairs available. Toilets.

Open: garden, all year, daily 9.30 – sunset. Visitor Centre and shop, 1 April to 16 October, daily 9.30 – 5.30. Licensed restaurant, same dates, Monday to Saturday 10 – 5, Sunday 10.30 – 5. Guided garden walks with head gardener, 1 April to 15 October, Monday to Friday at 1.30.

Admission: £3.00, children £1.50, adult/cruise parties £2.40, schools £1.20

Free entry for The National Trust for Scotland Members.

Kellie Castle Garden

Fife

On B9171, 3 miles north north-west of Pittenweem

A GARDEN made by Sir Robert Lorimer and subsequently restored by the Trust. Professor James Lorimer, Sir Robert's father, restored and made his home at Kellie Castle near Pittenweem, Fife. A delightful model of a late Victorian garden with box edged paths, rose arches and many herbaceous plants and roses of the period, representing a style not found in any other Trust garden. The castle is a fine example of the domestic architecture of the Lowland counties of Scotland in the 16th and 17th centuries. Video programme. Tearoom, Adventure Playground. Wheelchair access to garden. Induction loop for the hard of hearing.

Open: Castle, Good Friday to Easter Monday and 1 May to 23 October, daily 1.30 – 5.30; 9 to 30 April, Saturday/Sunday 1.30 – 5.30 (last admission 4.45). Garden and grounds, all year, daily 9.30 – sunset.

Admission: Castle and garden, adults £3.00, children £1.50, adult parties £2.40, schools £1.20, garden only (honesty box) £1.00.

Free entry for The National Trust for Scotland Members

Leith Hall Garden

Gordon, Grampian. On B9002, 1 mile west of Kennethmont and 34 miles north-west of Aberdeen

Priorwood Garden

Ettrick and Lauderdale, Borders A6091, in Melrose

THIS ATTRACTIVE old country house at Kennethmont, Grampian Region, the earliest part of which dates from 1650, was the home of the Leith and Leith-Hay families for more than three centuries. Exhibition on the Military Lairds of Leith Hall, entitled "For Crown and Country". Picnic area. The west garden was made by Mr and The Hon. Mrs Charles Leith-Hay around the beginning of the present century. The rock garden has recently been enhanced by The Scottish Garden Club in celebration of their 150th anniversary. Mr and Mrs Charles Leith-Hay also improved the garden, and instituted many other improvements to the policies. Their work was later continued by Mrs Leith-Hay's niece and her husband, Col. and Mrs Derrick Gascoigne. The property was given to the Trust by The Hon. Mrs Leith-Hay in 1945. Toilet for disabled.

Open: house, Good Friday to Easter Monday and 1 May to 30 September, daily 1.30 – 5.30 (last admission 4.45). Garden and grounds, all year, daily 9.30 – sunset.

Admission: house, adults £3.50, children £1.80, adult parties £2.80, schools £1.40. Garden and grounds £1.00 (honesty box).

Free entry for The National Trust for Scotland Members

THIS SMALL FORMAL GARDEN specialising in flowers for drying is situated in the middle of Melrose, Borders, adjacent to Melrose Abbey. Features include herbaceous border and beds of annual flowers suitable for drying. A wide range of information and drying aids, together with dried flowers from the garden, are on sale in the adjoining Trust Shop. Orchard walk. The property was purchased by the Trust in 1974.

Tourist Information Centre. Garden. NTS Shop and Dried-Flower Shop.

Open: 1 April to 24 December, Monday – Saturday 10 – 5.30, Sunday 1.30 – 5.30. Shop closed 31 October to 6 November for stocktaking. Opening may be delayed due to building works. Please contact property or regional office to confirm. Tel. Melrose (089 682) 2493 or (0592) 266566.

Admission: £1.00 (honesty box).

Best seen June to October.

Free entry for The National Trust for Scotland Members.

Pitmedden Garden

Gordon, Grampian. On A920, 1 mile west of Pitmedden village and 14 miles north of Aberdeen

AT PITMEDDEN, near Udny, in the Gordon District of Grampian Region, the National Trust for Scotland has re-created the 17th-century "Great Garden" originally laid out by Sir Alexander Seton, the first baronet of Pitmedden. Given to the Trust with an endowment from the late Major James Keith in 1951 and under the guidance of Dr James Richardson H.R.S.A., the formal parterres were re-created. Three of them from designs possibly used at Holyrood in Edinburgh and a fourth a tribute to the Setons, using the family crest and Scottish Heraldry. Fountains and sundials make excellent centrepieces to the garden filled with 40,000 annual flowers. The Museum of Farming Life from its early formation in 1980 has now grown to become one of the best exhibitions of Farming Life in the north-east. Extensive herbaceous borders, fruit trees and Herb Garden. Facilities for the disabled. Garden Room. Tearoom. Visitor Centre. Shop. Guided Tours available.

Open: Visitor Centre, museum, grounds and other facilities, 1 May to 30 September, daily 10 – 5.30 (last tour 5).

Admission: Garden and museum, adults £3.00, children £1.50, adult parties £2.40, schools £1.20.

Free entry for The National Trust for Scotland Members.

☷ The National Trust for Scotland
Threave Gardens
Stewartry, Dumfries and Galloway
Off A75, 1 mile west of Castle Douglas

THIS VICTORIAN MANSION HOUSE near Castle Douglas, Dumfries and Galloway Region, with policies, woodland and gardens extending in all to 1,490 acres, was presented to the Trust with an endowment in 1947 by the late Major A. F. Gordon of Threave. In 1960 the house was adapted for use as a school of horticulture. It caters for young people, between the ages of 17 and 21, who wish to make gardening their career. The course covers practical and theoretical gardening and allied subjects and is supported by Education Authorities.

Open: Garden, all year, daily 9.30 – sunset. Walled garden and glasshouses, all year, daily 9.30 – 5. Visitor Centre, exhibition and shop, 1 April to 23 October, daily 9.30 – 5.30. Restaurant, 10 – 5.

Admission: adults £3.00, children £1.50; adult parties £2.40, schools £1.20.

Free entry for The National Trust for Scotland Members.

HEAD GARDENERS' MEETING

Every summer the National Trust for Scotland arranges an annual meeting of Head Gardeners and other staff from Trust and privately owned gardens. The object is to enable gardeners to maintain contact with others in their profession and to keep up to date with recent technical developments. Meetings are normally based in university halls of residence throughout Scotland to allow visits to be made to gardens of interest in the area.

Garden owners who open under Scotland's Gardens Scheme are welcome to apply to send a member of their staff. Please ask for further details from Gardens Department, The National Trust for Scotland, 5 Charlotte Square, Edinburgh EH2 4DU, telephone 031-226 5922.

☙ The National Trust for Scotland
OTHER TRUST GARDEN PROPERTIES
(Free entry for The National Trust for Scotland Members)

BALMACARA, ROSS AND CROMARTY
The woodland garden at Lochalsh House was begun in 1979 and will take many years to complete. There are magnificent mature trees, but it is still a garden in the making. Open all year, daily 9.30 – sunset. Admission: adults £1.00, children 50p.

BRODIE CASTLE, MORAY
A garden being restored to include a selection of the Brodie collection of daffodils and other varieties. Interesting mature trees and avenue. Castle open 1 April to 25 September, Monday to Saturday 11 – 5.30, Sunday 1.30 – 5.30 (last admission 4.30); 1 to 16 October, Saturday 11 – 5.30, Sunday 1.30 – 5.30 (last admission 4.30). Other times by appointment. Grounds, all year, daily 9.30 – sunset. Admission: Castle, adults £3.50, children £1.80; adult parties £2.80; schools £1.40. Grounds £1.00 (honesty box).

CASTLE FRASER, ABERDEENSHIRE
A landscaped park with good trees and a walled garden which has been redesigned in a formal manner, in keeping with the Castle. Open: Castle, 1 May to 30 June and 1 to 30 September, daily 1.30 – 5.30; 1 July to 31 August daily 11 – 5.30; 1 to 9 October, Saturday/Sunday 1.30 – 5.30 (last admission 5). Garden and grounds, all year, daily 9.30 – sunset. Admission: Castle, adults £3.50, children £1.80; adult parties £2.80; schools £1.40. Grounds £1.00 (honesty box).

DRUM CASTLE, ABERDEENSHIRE
Interesting parkland containing a fascinating collection of trees, 100 acre Wood of Drum and Arboretum. Castle open Good Friday to Easter Monday, 1 May to 30 June and 1 to 30 September, daily 1.30 – 5.30; 1 July to 31 August daily 11 – 5.30; 1 to 9 October, Saturday/Sunday 1.30 – 5.30 (last admission 4.45). Garden, 1 May to 9 October, daily 10 – 6. Grounds all year, daily 9.30 – sunset. Admission: Castle, garden and grounds adults £3.50, children £1.80; adult parties £2.80; schools £1.40. Grounds, adults £1.50, children 80p. Group visits must be pre-booked.

FYVIE CASTLE, ABERDEENSHIRE
Parkland with superb walks around ornamental loch. Castle open Good Friday to Easter Monday, 1 May to 30 June and 1 to 30 September, daily 1.30 – 5.30; 1 July to 31 August daily 11 – 5.30; 1 to 9 October, Saturday/Sunday 1.30 – 5.30 (last admission 4.45). Tearoom, dates as Castle, but opens 12.30 when Castle opens 1.30. Grounds all year, daily 9.30 – sunset. Admission: Castle, adults £3.50, children £1.80; adult parties £2.80; schools £1.40, Grounds £1.00 (honesty box).

GREENBANK GARDEN, CLARKSTON, GLASGOW
A Gardening Advice Centre offering a series of regular guided walks. Garden with an excellent collection of shrub roses. Programme of events available on request. Special garden for the disabled. Garden open all year (except 25/26 December and 1/2 January), daily 9.30 – sunset. Admission: adults £2.00, children £1.00; adult parties £1.60; schools 80p.

HADDO HOUSE, ABERDEENSHIRE
A formal garden, adjoining the Country Park. Open all year. Formal rose garden and borders. House open Good Friday to Easter Monday, 1 May to 30 June and 1 to 30 September, daily 1.30 – 5.30; 1 July to 31 August daily 11 – 5.30; 1 to 9 October, Saturday/Sunday 1.30 – 5.30 (last admission 4.45); Shop and Stables Restaurant, 1 April to 30 September, daily 11 – 5.30; 1 to 9 October Saturday/Sunday 11 – 5.30. Garden and Country Park all year, daily 9.30 – sunset. Admission: Castle adults £3.50, children £1.80; adult parties £2.80; schools £1.40. Grounds £1.00 (honesty box).

HOUSE OF DUN, MONTROSE, ANGUS
Restoration of the gardens are based largely on designs originally conceived by Lady Augusta using typical plants of the 1840s. Upgrading of the woodlands and their former footpaths is also being carried out. Open: house, courtyard and restaurant, Good Friday to Easter Monday and 1 May to 30 September, daily 11 – 5.30; 1 to 23 October, Saturday/Sunday 11 – 5.30 (last admission to house 5). Coaches by appointment only. Garden and grounds, all year, daily 9.30 – sunset. Admission: adults £3.50, children £1.80; adult parties £2.80; schools £1.40. Grounds £1.00 (honesty box).

MALLENY HOUSE GARDEN, BALERNO, EDINBURGH
This 17th-century house (not open to the public) has a delightfully personal garden with many interesting plants and features, and a particularly good collection of shrub roses. National Bonsai collection for Scotland. Open all year, daily 9.30 – sunset. Admission: £1.00 (honesty box).

☙ The National Trust for Scotland
23 Beautiful Gardens to Visit

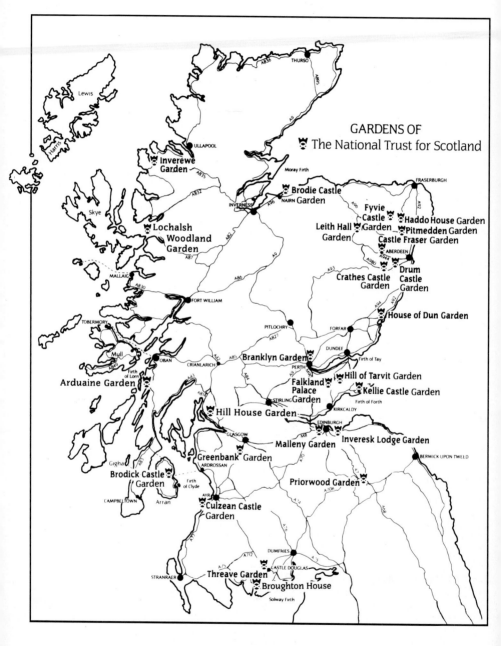

GARDENS OF
☙ The National Trust for Scotland

Inverewe Garden

Brodie Castle Garden

Fyvie Castle

Haddo House Garden

Leith Hall Garden

Pitmedden Garden

Lochalsh Woodland Garden

Castle Fraser Garden

Drum Castle Garden

Crathes Castle Garden

House of Dun Garden

Branklyn Garden

Hill of Tarvit Garden

Arduaine Garden

Falkland Palace Garden

Kellie Castle Garden

Hill House Garden

Malleny Garden

Inveresk Lodge Garden

Greenbank Garden

Brodick Castle Garden

Priorwood Garden

Culzean Castle Garden

Threave Garden

Broughton House

♛ The National Trust for Scotland
All that we do, we do for you

THE NATIONAL TRUST FOR SCOTLAND belongs to you—to the people who love Scotland—and opens its properties for the enjoyment of all. That's why the brooding magnificence of Glen Coe, the soaring mountains of Kintail, the peaceful beaches of Iona and so many great gardens are there for all to see and enjoy, protected for posterity.

At Inverewe Garden, where palm trees grow on the same latitude as Labrador, or Brodick Castle Garden where the rhododendrons win prizes at flower shows on both sides of the Atlantic, and in our gardens throughout Scotland, 30 young gardeners are now being trained. And at Threave School of Horticulture, we run a two-year residential course for the head gardeners of the future.

At Culzean Castle, Robert Adam's masterpiece overlooking the Clyde, the stonework is eroded by time and needs continual restoration. Repairs to the viaduct, and many other buildings on the estate now in progress, will take a team of stonemasons several years to complete. And the contents of our properties require as much attention and painstaking care as the exteriors. The Trust has its own bookbinding, metalwork, picture-framing and furniture restoration workshops.

But maintaining properties costs money. Gardens need replanting, curtains frayed with age require to be repaired, and paths on mountains worn by countless feet need re-seeding. We repair leaky roofs, antiquated plumbing and rusting suits of armour. The list is endless. Each year it costs the Trust almost £14m to carry out this work, quite apart from any new projects we may wish to undertake. That's why we need your help.

If you love the countryside and have a special place in your heart for Scotland, you can help its preservation by joining the National Trust for Scotland. On the next page you will find another six good reasons for joining.

♛ The National Trust for Scotland

Benefits of Membership

WE DONT ASK FOR MUCH: we believe that we give so much in return. For example the cost of a single membership for a 12-month period is £23.00 and a whole family can join for £38.00—less than an average family night out.

In exchange we give you:

1 Free admission to over 100 properties in Scotland, plus over 300 properties of The National Trust, a completely separate organisation, in England, Wales and Northern Ireland.

2 Our quarterly colour magazine, *Heritage Scotland*, with lists of events, winter activities and a host of opportunities for you to enjoy.

3 Details of our Cruises, Guided Walks and Ranger/Naturalist programmes. And, for those who would like to do a little more, details of how to join one of our Members' support groups.

4 Priority booking for our holiday cottages, adventure base camps for groups, St Kilda work parties, Thistle camps for young people and our caravan parks and campsites.

5 Our annual illustrated *Guide to Over 100 Properties* listing opening times and facilities, together with our *Annual Report*.

6 Facilities at our properties for all the family—grandparents, parents and children—including shops with our specially designed range of goods—and tearooms when you need to take the weight off your feet.

The National Trust for Scotland is a charity, independent of Government, supported by 235,000 members

JOIN Scotland's leading conservation organisation

Membership Enrolment Form   Rates valid until 31 October 1994

- ☐ <u>Ordinary:</u> £23.00 or more per annum.
- ☐ <u>Family:</u> £38.00 or more per annum. Two adults at one address (and any of their children, under 18).
- ☐ <u>Life:</u> £460.00 or more (includes cardholder's children under 18).
- ☐ <u>Junior:</u> £10.00 or more per annum (23 yrs and under).   Date of birth __/__/__

<u>Pensioners:</u> (over 60 and retired) may join at concessionary rates as
        Ordinary members £12.00 ☐
        Family members £19.00 ☐
        Life members £230.00 ☐

I enclose remittance for/please charge my Credit Card £_____ Expiry date __/__

Visa/Access/American Express/Switch No: ☐☐☐☐ ☐☐☐☐ ☐☐☐☐ ☐☐☐☐

Please print

Mr/Mrs/Miss/Ms Surname_____Initials_____

Address:_____

_____

_____Postcode:_____

FOR NTS USE ONLY		
MEMBERSHIP NO.		
	TYPE	SOURCE
		214
DAY	MONTH	YEAR
Amount received		
£		

Please send to: Membership Services, The National Trust for Scotland, 5 Charlotte Square, Edinburgh EH2 4DU

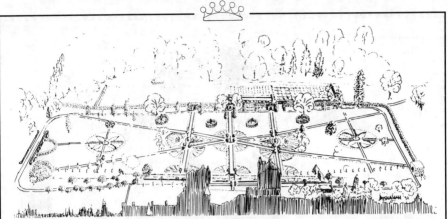

DRUMMOND CASTLE GARDENS
CRIEFF, PERTHSHIRE

Scotland's largest formal gardens, said to be among the finest in Europe. The upper terraces overlook a magnificent Victorian parterre, and the famous sundial by John Milne, master mason to Charles I, has been the centrepiece since 1630.

OPEN MAY TO SEPTEMBER DAILY 2pm - 6pm (last entry 5pm)

Entrance 2 miles south of Crieff on the A822

Telephone (0764) 681257

Dougal Philip's

WALLED GARDEN CENTRE
at Hopetoun House
South Queensferry, West Lothian

Set in four acres of the walled garden full of ideas and unusual plants for your garden. You will also discover probably the widest selection of hardy plants available for sale in Scotland.

Our knowledgeable and friendly staff will be pleased to welcome you and help with your enquiries.

Relax in this beautiful setting and enjoy the Potting-Shed Tearoom.

Easy Car Parking
Free Admission to Walled Garden
Open Daily 10-5.30 pm

031-319 1122

Bring this advert for a
FREE ENTRY
to our Raffle Draw
on Open Day
May 15th

145

TWO 6-DAY COACH TOURS OF HOUSES AND GARDENS IN 1994

YORKSHIRE 12 - 17 MAY
FIFE & KINROSS 19 - 24 JUNE

Every year we run two 6-day tours to visit many beautiful privately owned gardens which open for charity.
We stay for five nights in a good standard hotel starting and ending the tour in Edinburgh.

Please write for a brochure to:
The General Organiser
Scotland's Gardens Scheme
31 Castle Terrace, Edinburgh EH1 2EL

151

Springtime in The Borders and Argyll and Bute
Two Garden Festivals in May – Fun for all the family!

A Festival Weekend at Kailzie Gardens, Peebles (on B7062)
7th and 8th May 1994

A host of activities including:

Grand Opening of New Trout Pond

Fishing Competitions and Casting Demonstrations

Fete

Garden Workshops

Cookery Demonstrations

Trade and Craft Stands

Falconry Display

Many Activities for Children

Programme details available from mid-March 1994
Telephone 0721 720007

The First Argyll and Bute Gardens Festival
Opening Weekend at Crarae Gardens
(12 miles south of Inveraray on A83)
21st and 22nd May 1994

Plant Workshops	Falconry Display
Cooking Demonstration by Sue Lawrence	Plant Sales
	Flower Arranging Demonstration
Chainsaw Carving	Photographic Exhibition
Garden Exhibits	Ceilidh with Pipes and Dancing

Argyll & the Islands
ENTERPRISE

Programme of Events and details of other gardens open in Argyll and Bute during the Festival can be obtained from Crarae Visitor Centre

Telephone 0546 86614

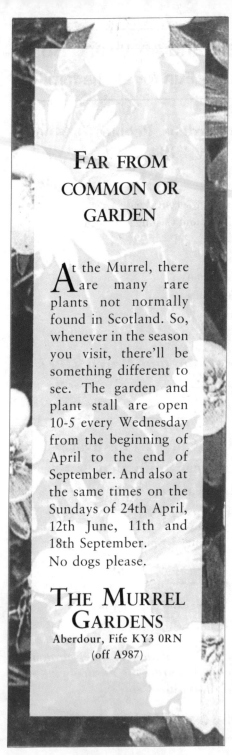

FAR FROM COMMON OR GARDEN

At the Murrel, there are many rare plants not normally found in Scotland. So, whenever in the season you visit, there'll be something different to see. The garden and plant stall are open 10-5 every Wednesday from the beginning of April to the end of September. And also at the same times on the Sundays of 24th April, 12th June, 11th and 18th September.

No dogs please.

THE MURREL GARDENS
Aberdour, Fife KY3 0RN
(off A987)

BRIGHTWATER HOLIDAYS

Quality Garden Tours

Scotland's Royal Gardens
10 – 12 June 1994   3 days   £135

Based at the 3-star Park Hotel, Montrose. Visits include Falkland Palace, Balmoral Castle, Glamis Castle, Crathes Castle, Scone Palace, House of Pitmuies.

Scotland's Alpine Gardens
10 - 13 June 1994   4 days   £165
£30 single supplement

Based at the 3-star Station Hotel, Perth. Visits include Branklyn, Henry Taylor's Gardens, House of Pitmuies, Cluny House, Ben Lawers, St Andrews Botanic Gardens.

Monet's Garden and the Gardens of Normandy
8 – 12 July 1994   5 days   £245

Based in Rouen Ibis Hotel. Visits include gardens of Claude Monet at Giverny, Arboretum d'Harcourt, Gertrude Jekyll's Parc Floral Les Montiers.

All Tours include:
➢ **Luxury coaching throughout from various pick-up points**
➢ **Service of a tour guide**
➢ **Dinner, bed and breakfast in rooms with full private facilities**

For brochure of these and other garden tours contact:

Brightwater Holidays
Eden Park House, Cupar
Fife KY15 4HS
Tel: 0334 657155
ABTOT NO. 5001

☆ A fully bonded tour operator ☆

156

THE BUCCLEUCH ESTATES
invite you to visit

BOWHILL HOUSE & COUNTRY PARK, Nr Selkirk (Scottish Borders)

18/19th century house in beautiful countryside. Outstanding art collection, fine French furniture and relics of Duke of Monmouth, Sir Walter Scott and Queen Victoria.

Exciting Adventure Woodland Play Area. Visitor Centre. Nature Trails. Picnic Areas. Riding Centre (Selkirk 20192). Mountain Bicycle Hire (0721 20336). Restored Victorian Kitchen. Audio-Visual. Tea Room. Gift Shop.

OPEN 1994

House	1-31 July daily 1-4.30
Country Park	1st Saturday in May to late Summer Bank Holiday (UK) daily except Fridays 12-5. Open on Fridays during July with House.
Telephone No.	Selkirk (0750) 20732.

Off A708—St. Mary's Loch-Moffat Road 3 miles west of Selkirk. Edinburgh 42 miles, Glasgow 75 miles, Berwick 43 miles, Newcastle 80 miles, Carlisle 56 miles.

Bowhill House

BOUGHTON HOUSE, Nr Kettering (Northamptonshire)

Northamptonshire home of the Dukes of Buccleuch and their Montagu ancestors since 1528. Important art collection, French and English Furniture and Tapestries. "A vision of Louis XIV's Versailles transported to England".

Exciting Adventure Woodland Play Area. Nature Trail. Tea Room. Gift Shop. Garden Centre.

OPEN 1994

Grounds	1st May-1st October, 1-5 daily except Fridays.
House and Grounds	1 August-1 September, 2-5 daily. (Grounds open 1 p.m.).
Telephone No.	Kettering (0536) 515731.

Off A43, 3 miles north of Kettering. Northampton 17 miles, Cambridge 45 miles, Coventry 44 miles, Peterborough 32 miles, Leicester 26 miles, London 50 minutes by train.

Boughton House

DRUMLANRIG CASTLE & COUNTRY PARK Nr Thornhill, Dumfriesshire (South-west Scotland)

Castle built 1679-91 on a 15th century Douglas stronghold. Set in parkland ringed by wild hills. French furniture. Paintings by Rembrandt, Holbein and Leonardo. Bonnie Prince Charlie relics. Gift shop. Tea Room. Exciting Adventure Woodland Play Area. Picnic Site. Nature Trails. Birds of Prey Centre. Visitors Centre. Craft Centre.

OPEN 1994

Castle and Country Park	Saturday 30 April to Monday 29 August daily 11-5, Sundays 1-5. Castle closed Thursday. Last entry to Castle 4 p.m.
Telephone Nos.	Thornhill (0848) 330248 (Castle). Thornhill (0848) 331555 (Country Park).

Off A76, 4 miles north of Thornhill. Glasgow 56 miles, Dumfries 18 miles, Edinburgh 56 miles, Carlisle 51 miles.

Drumlanrig Castle

DALKEITH PARK, Nr Edinburgh (Lothian Region)

Dalkeith Palace not open to public

Nature Trails. Woodland and riverside walks in the extensive grounds of Dalkeith Palace. Tunnel Walk. Adam Bridge. Fascinating Architecture.

Exciting Adventure Woodland Play Area. Picnic Area. Barbecue facilities. Information Centre. Birds of Prey flying demonstration. Scottish farm animals. Cart rides. Ranger service.

OPEN 1994

Grounds	26 March-29 October, 10 a.m.-6 p.m. daily.
Telephone Nos.	031-663 5684 or 031-665 3277.

Access from east end of Dalkeith High Street.

Off A68, 3 miles from Edinburgh City Boundary.

Dalkeith Palace from the Nature Trail

Parties welcome at all these estates (Special terms and extended opening times for pre-booked parties over 20).
All the houses have special facilities for wheelchair visitors.

Finlaystone

Overlooking the Clyde
10 min. west of Glasgow Airport on A8 west of Langbank

Beautiful Gardens: Woodland walks with waterfalls, picnic and play areas, visitors' centre with Celtic art exhibition
OPEN THROUGHOUT THE YEAR 10.30 - 5.00
Lunch and Tea in "Celtic Tree" in Walled Garden (closed winter weekdays)
Historic house with doll collection and Victorian kitchen. Open Sundays April-August 2.30-4.30 or by appointment
Group Bookings Welcome

Tel. Mrs G. MacMillan, Langbank (0475) 540 285
or Ranger, Langbank (0475) 540 505

Drumcruilton Thornhill

Friendly, Comfortable, Farmhouse Accommodation

Outstanding Scenic Position, close to all Fishing

B & B / E.M. and packed lunches

For brochure contact:

MRS D. HILL,
DRUMCRUILTON, THORNHILL
DUMFRIESSHIRE DG3 5BG

08485 210

BARGANY, AYRSHIRE

Woodland garden with fine trees, early spring flowers, and shrubs. Rock gardens and Lily pond surrounded by rhododendrons and azaleas flowering in May and June. Outstanding autumn colours. Easy paths and walks.

**Open daily 10 a.m. – 7 p.m. (4 p.m. in winter)
from March 1 to October 31**

Situated in the Valley of Girvan Water, 4 miles from Girvan, 18 miles South of Ayr on Route B734 Girvan to Dailly.

*Bus parties by arrangement with
John Dalrymple Hamilton*

Telephone: 0465 3365

SCOTLAND'S GARDENS 1995

To: **The General Organiser
Scotland's Gardens Scheme
31 Castle Terrace
Edinburgh
EH1 2EL**

I would be interested to receive a copy of "Scotland's Gardens 1995" when it is available (mid-Feb) and enclose a cheque/P.O. for £3.00 which includes P&P.

Name _____

Address _____

_____

_____

Torosay Castle

Craignure, Isle of Mull

Telephone: 06802 421

Torosay is a beautiful family home, designed by eminent architect David Bryce in 1858.

It is surrounded by 12 acres of varied and spectacular gardens, including formal terraces (attributed to Sir Robert Lorimer) and Statue Walk surrounded by less formal woodland and water garden, Eucalyptus walk, Japanese garden and rockery, making a fine setting for many interesting plants. This splendid garden is offset by spectacular views past Duart Castle and the Sound of Mull to the mountains of Appin and Lorne.

A full day out is completed by a visit to the Isle of Mull Weavers and a trip on the Mull Narrow Gauge Railway, nearby.

Castle and Gardens open May to Mid October, 10.30-5.00.
Tearoom, giftshop, partial access for the disabled.
Gardens only, open all year.

Getting there:
By MacBrayne's ferry from Oban to Craignure,
then by train, car or Forest Walk (1$\frac{1}{2}$ miles).
By ferry Lochaline-Fishnish (7 miles).
Or by motor launch Maid of the Firth from Oban Esplanade, for a short visit.

FLOORS CASTLE
KELSO

Scotland's largest inhabited Castle. Gardens and parks overlooking the River Tweed and Cheviot Hills. Splendid herbaceous border.
Pipe Bands and Highland Dancers: 1 and 29 May, 19 June, 17 July
Massed Pipe Bands: 28 August 1994

Open Easter and from 24 April, May, June, Sept: Sun to Thurs 10.30am to 5.30pm.
July, August: Open daily 10.30am to 5.30pm.   October: Sun and Wed 10.30am to 4.30pm

Enquiries: Roxburghe Estates Office, Kelso, TD5 7SF. Telephone: (0573) 223333

VISIT THE ST ANDREWS BOTANIC GARDEN

Rock, peat and water gardens, tree, shrub, bulb and herbaceous borders. Wide range of plants.

OPEN
7 days a week from April to October.
10 a.m. to 4 p.m. April and October.
10 a.m. to 7 p.m. from May to September.
From November to March weekdays only 10 a.m. to 4 p,m,
Glasshouses 11 a.m. to 3.30 p.m. weekdays only.

ENTRY CHARGES
£1   Children under 16 and senior citizens 50p.

DOBBIES

EDINBURGH BUTTERFLY AND INSECT WORLD

Stroll through the wonderful world of a tropical rainforest setting, landscaped with exotic plants, waterfalls and pools, and see hundreds of spectacular, free-flying butterflies from all over the world!

See too the fascinating leaf cutting ants, tarantulas, stick insects and honey bee display.

Visit our unusual gift shop and enjoy a coffee in Dobbies tea room.

OPEN 12 MARCH TO 8 JANUARY FROM 10 AM—SEVEN DAYS A WEEK

GLENDOICK GARDEN CENTRE
—— *TAYSIDE'S PREMIER PLANT CENTRE* ——

* Our display beds are full of **ALPINES, HERBACEOUS** and **SHRUBS**
* Extensive range of **TREES, FRUIT** and **CONIFERS**
* **RHODODENDRONS** and **AZALEAS** are our speciality, we have a very good selection on show. Sometimes larger specimens are available

In our new Display Garden you will find a wide range of plants which may give you some inspiration for your own garden

We are open seven days a week 9am – 6pm. 8 miles from Perth, 14 miles from Dundee on what was the A85 now the A90.   Tel: 0738 86260

161

162

Scotland's Gardens Scheme

H O L I D A Y S

Three fully inclusive special Garden Tours organised for Scotland's Gardens Scheme by Brightwater Holidays

Highland and Island Gardens

HIGHLAND & ISLAND GARDENS
19 - 22 April 1994
£215 per person
£12 single room supplement.
Based at the 4 Star Stonefield Castle Hotel,
Escorted throughout by Peter Clough
- Head gardener of Inverewe Gardens.
Our Spring tour visits the magnificent western seaboard of Scotland including Arkinglas Gardens, Crarae Gardens, Achamore Gardens on Gigha, Brodick Castle Gardens on Arran, and Arduaine Gardens.
Pick Up Points:-   Perth   Kinross   Edinburgh   Glasgow.

THE CHELSEA FLOWER SHOW
including the ROMANCE OF SISSINGHURST GARDENS.

26 - 30 May 1994
Price £225
Single room supplement £32 per person.
Based at the 3 Star Great Danes Hotel, Maidstone.
A classic garden tour visiting the finest gardens of England and the finest flower show in the World.
Visits include; Arley Hall in Cheshire,
all day visit to the Chelsea Flower Show (ticket included),
Wisley Gardens, Great Comp Gardens,
Sissinghurst Gardens, and Bridgemere Garden World.
Pick Up Points: Perth   Kinross   Edinburgh   Glasgow.

The Chelsea Flower Show

Gardens of the far north

GARDENS OF THE FAR NORTH
1 - 3 September 1994
£139 per person
£10 single room supplement.
Based at the 3 star Garve Hotel near Strathpeffer.
The Far North of Scotland offers spectacular,
wild and beautiful scenery, even in this most remote
region you will find enchanting gardens, inlcuding
the rare opportunity to visit the Queen Mother's
garden at the Castle of Mey (open under the auspices
of Scotland's Gardens Scheme). Tour includes;
Cluny Gardens in Aberfeldy, Alpine nursery of Jack Drake's
Dunrobin Castle Gardens, Castle of Mey Gardens, Inverewe Gardens
Pick Up Points: Glasgow   Edinburgh   Kinross   Perth.   Dumfries

For brochure and full details contact:-SGS Tours c/o Brightwater Holidays,
Eden Park House, Cupar, Fife KY154HS. Tel 0334 657155
ABTOT No 5001
-A fully bonded tour operator for your financial protection-

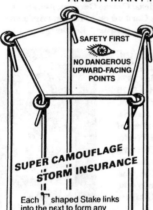

164

INDEX TO GARDENS

INDEX TO ADVERTISERS